GW00320387

Monk Jianzhen's Journey to Japan

鉴真东渡弘法

乐　敏　邓荫柯　编著

Translated by Chang Guojie

五洲传播出版社
China Intercontinental Press

图书在版编目（CIP）数据

鉴真东渡弘法：汉英对照/乐敏，邓荫柯编著；畅国杰译.—北京：五洲传播出版社，2010.1

ISBN 978-7-5085-1705-6

I.①鉴… II.①乐… ②邓… ③畅… III.①鉴真（688～763）–生平事迹–汉、英 ②中日关系–文化交流–文化史–汉、英 IV.①K203 ②K313.03

中国版本图书馆CIP数据核字（2009）第192566号

中外文化交流故事丛书（Roads to the World）

顾　　问：赵启正　沈锡麟　潘　岳
　　　　　周黎明（美）李　莎（加）威廉·林赛（英）
主　　编：荆孝敏　邓锦辉
编 著 者：乐　敏　邓荫柯
翻　　译：世纪英信·畅国杰
责任编辑：邓锦辉
设计指导：田　林
封面绘画：李　骐
设计制作：北京尚捷时迅文化艺术有限公司
图　　片：乐　敏　田建国　TBS　张　恕 Fotoe

鉴真东渡弘法
Monk Jianzhen's Journey to Japan

出版发行　五洲传播出版社（北京市海淀区北小马厂6号 邮编：100038）
电　　话　8610-58891281（发行部）
网　　址　www.cicc.org.cn
承 印 者　北京外文印务有限公司
版　　次　2010年1月第1版第1次印刷
开　　本　720×965毫米 1/16
印　　张　10.25
定　　价　78.00元

Contents 目 录

FOREWORD

It has been a long and exciting history of tremendous cultural exchange between China and other countries. In terms of culture, economy, ideology, and personnel, these exchanges between China and other countries can be dated back to the times of Qin and Han dynasties—directly or indirectly, by land or sea. The long-term and multi-faceted cultural exchange helps the world to understand more about China and the rest of the world, enriching the common wealth of mankind—both materially and spiritually.

The book series entitled *Roads to the World* offers the most splendid stories in the entire history of Sino-foreign cultural exchange. We hereby offer them to foreign students learning the Chinese language, and to foreign readers who have a keen interest in Chinese culture. These stories depict important personalities, events, and phenomena in various fields of cultural exchange between China and other nations, and among different peoples. By reading the books, you may understand China and Chinese civilization profoundly, and the close link between Chinese civilization and other civilizations of the world. The books highlight the efforts and contributions of Chinese people and Chinese civilization in the world's cultural interchange. They reflect mankind's common spiritual pursuit and the orientation of values.

This book tells the story of Jianzhen—a prominent monk, who lived during the Tang Dynasty times in China. He went through many hardships making six attempts to cross the sea to take the Buddhist precepts to Japan. He succeeded in his last attempt. He introduced the advanced culture of the Tang Dynasty (architecture, sculpture, calligraphy, painting, and traditional Chinese medicine) to Japan, which still fuels the development of Japanese culture. The Japanese conferred him with the title "Cultural Benefactor." He stands high as the symbol of long-term Sino-Japanese cultural exchange!

前　言

　　中国与其他国家、民族之间的文化交流具有悠久而曲折的历史。在中国与外国之间，通过间接的和直接的、陆路的和海路的、有形的和无形的多种渠道，各种文化、经济、思想、人员方面的交流，可以上溯至秦汉时代，下及于当今社会。长期的、多方面的交流，增进了中国与其他国家、民族之间的了解，使人类的共同财富（物质的和精神的）更加丰富。

　　中外文化交流故事丛书（Roads to the World）的宗旨，是从中外文化交流的历史长河中，选择那些最璀璨的明珠，通过讲故事的方式，介绍给学习汉语的外国学生和对中国文化感兴趣的外国读者。这些故事描述中国与其他国家、民族在各个领域文化交流中的重要人物、事件和现象，以使外国读者能够更深入地理解中国，理解中国文明，理解中国文明与其他各文明之间的密切关系，以及中国人和中国文明在这种交流过程中所作出的努力和贡献，并尽力彰显人类共同的精神追求与价值取向。

本书讲述的是唐代高僧鉴真和尚历尽艰辛，东渡日本、弘传佛法的故事。鉴真大师还将建筑、雕塑、书法、绘画、医药等先进的中华文化传播到异邦，促进了日本文化的发展，被称为日本的"文化恩人"。其本人也成为源远流长的中日文化交流的象征。

I

Great Buddhism Master

Jianzhen (Ganjin)—a renowned Vinaya master of the Tang Dynasty of China (618–907)—underwent many hardships during six attempts to sail eastwards to Japan. The first five ended in failure due to many reasons, but he finally made it in his last attempt. He reached Japan in year 754 and devoted rest of his life to disseminating Buddhist doctrines. As a great cultural envoy, he made splendid contributions to the cultural exchange and development between China and Japan with wisdom and effort. He set a permanent example to the world with his firm faith, indomitable will and broadmindedness.

Jianzhen was born to a devout Buddhist family in year 688 in Jiangyang County, Yangzhou (now eastern suburb of Yangzhou, Jiangsu Province) in the reign of Express Wu Zetian (690–705). His surname was Chunyu. His father was a rich businessman, and family was well off. As a devout believer in Buddhism, his father learned Zen and received ordination too. With a Buddhist shrine at home,

1

江淮独秀

鉴真和尚是中国唐朝（618—907）时候的一位佛教高僧，他历尽磨难，经历了五次失败，终于在754年东渡日本，弘传佛法。作为一位伟大的文化使者，他将智慧、心血和生命都贡献给了中日文化交流事业，为世人树立了坚定信仰、顽强意志和博大胸怀的不朽典范。

鉴真像。日本奈良唐招提寺御影堂藏。田建国供图。
The portrait of Jianzhen, collected in Mieido (Portrait Hall), Tōshōdai-ji Temple, Nara, Japan. Photo credit: Tian Jianguo.

鉴真本姓淳于，于688年生于扬州东郊的江阳县。鉴真的父亲是一位富商，家境殷实，而且笃信佛

his father paid respect to the Buddha and chanted sutras every day. When Jianzhen was a little boy, his father often told him Buddhist tales and took him to worship and offer incense in temples and monasteries. To his father's happiness, the little boy showed no interest in the luxurious life in Yangzhou. Jianzhen had great enthusiasm in religion

扬州大明寺栖灵塔。阿南史代摄。
Qiling Pagoda in Daming Temple, Yangzhou. Photo by Virginia Anami.

and culture. He had the nature of Buddha and yearned for living in a strong religious and cultural environment.

Jianzhen and his father were quite familiar with the abbot of the Dayun Temple in Yangzhou—Master Zhiman. With kind and elegant attitudes, the master left little Jianzhen with a carefree and happy feeling. Tranquil environment in the temple, lofty majestic halls, serene smiles on the faces of Buddha statues, long deep sound of chanting sutras, and stories about Buddhist willingness to do good and boundless kindness and virtue—all these deeply attracted Jianzhen. He began to get fascinated with

扬州运河两岸的古建筑。Fotoe供图。
Historic buildings near the banks of the Grand Canal, Yangzhou. Photo credit: Fotoe.

教，曾经学禅受戒，家中设有佛堂，礼佛诵经是每日必做的功课。他常常给小鉴真讲解佛经故事，领鉴真去寺庙进香拜佛。小鉴真对扬州的灯红酒绿、车水马龙没有什么兴趣，却对浓厚的宗教文化氛围心有灵犀，心向往之。鉴真父子与大云寺的住持智满法师十分熟悉，法师亲切文雅的态度，给了小鉴真轻松而快乐的感觉。寺院清幽静谧的环境，巍峨庄严的殿堂，安详微笑的佛像，悠长深沉的诵经之声，佛教徒乐善好施、功德无量的故事，都深深吸引着小鉴真。他开

Yangzhou

Yangzhou in Jiangsu Province of East China is located in the north wing of the Yangtze River Delta. Yangzhou was the third largest metropolis—only second to the capital of Chang'an (now Xi'an) and eastern capital of Luoyang during the Tang Dynasty. It was a leading economic and cultural center and major port of foreign trade and external exchange since the Tang Dynasty rule. The Grand Canal built during the Sui Dynasty (581–618), ran through both Luoyang and Yangzhou, making Yangzhou the north-south, west-east water and land transport hub. The transport system was well developed in Yangzhou where many merchants and foreigners gathered. The Buddhist culture flourished there.

Buddhism and gradually cherished a desire to become an eminent monk to accumulate kindness and virtue and transmit Buddhist precepts among the common people for the rest of his life.

One day in year 702, when he was 14 years old, Jianzhen asked his father for permission to leave home and become a monk in the Dayun Temple. As the father understood the child's zeal that temple visits had awakened his son, he agreed to his son's request and invited Master Zhiman as his son's mentor. Knowing that Jianzhen had a profound wisdom, Zhiman gladly

扬州

扬州今属中国东部的江苏省，位于长江三角洲北翼。盛唐时代，扬州是仅次于首都长安（今陕西西安）和东都洛阳的大都市，是中国与各国通商贸易和文化交流的主要口岸之一，以及海上丝绸之路重要的港口城市。建于隋朝（581—618）的大运河连接洛阳与扬州，使扬州成为南北、东西水陆交通的总枢纽。这里交通发达，商贾云集，外国人众多，而且佛教文化兴盛。

始迷恋佛法，逐渐萌发出了要做一个积善积德、普度众生的大德高僧的心愿。

702年，14岁的鉴真向父亲表达了去大云寺出家为僧的愿望。父亲早就感觉到这个孩子有不浅的佛缘，就欣然答应了他的请求，而且请求智满法师做他的师父。智满法师也看出鉴真慧根深厚，相信他日后必有大成就，便欣然收他为徒。父亲深知佛寺的规矩，就对鉴真说，你先做"行者"吧，不剃发，在寺庙里服劳役。小小的鉴真以超出一个孩子的自觉一心向佛，

accepted him as a disciple. The master believed that
Jianzhen would become a mahasiddha (a Buddhist
with great spiritual accomplishment) in the future. His
father knew monastic disciplines and rules very well.
He told Jianzhen to start as a "novice" at the temple.
Initially, Jianzhen had hair and worked as a servant
and lay laborer. With his great awareness, this little boy
focused on paying respect to Buddhism, industriously
performed all the chores, such as sweeping the imperial
courtyard, washing the master's chamber pot and
kasaya (cassock or robe), and often reading Buddhist
scriptures and teachings until midnight. The sangha at
the temple liked him very much. He successfully passed
the examination held by the imperial court and got an
official permit to become a monk and join a monastery
as scheduled. The Daming Temple held a grand tonsure
ceremony and a public ordination ceremony for him.
After that, he became a samanera (little monk) with a
monastic title (Buddhist name) of Jianzhen. At that time,
becoming a member of the sangha was a very honorable
thing due to the imperial court's advocacy and the
public recognition. It cost more money to receive a
precept-granting ceremony and to get an official permit
for becoming a Buddhist monk or nun. It was very
difficult for an ordinary family to afford. It was evident
that Jianzhen grew up in a rich family. Jianzhen devoted

唐代扬州古城墙遗址。阿南史代摄。
The historic site of ancient city wall of Yangzhou. Photo by Virginia Anami.

勤劳地做一切杂事，诸如洒扫庭除、洗涤师父的溺器和袈裟等，而且苦读经书，常常到深夜才熄灯，寺里上上下下都喜欢他。等到官府度僧的日期一到，他便顺利通过了考核，领到了度牒，也就是国家向僧尼发放的身份证明文件。寺里很快为他举行了隆重的剃度仪式，取法名鉴真，授沙弥戒。在当时，由于朝廷的倡导和民众的认同，进入佛门是一件很有荣耀的事，受戒和领取度牒所需要的费用也日益攀高，不是普通家庭所能负担的。由此足见鉴真的家境相当富裕。像

himself to Buddhism without taking into account the livelihood, but purely due to his lofty faith and firm determination.

Jianzhen studied Buddhism at the Dayun Temple. Despite being a highly intelligent learner, he spared no efforts to study all the doctrines, sutras, and Buddhist disciplines. Under the careful guidance of Master Zhiman, he gained much knowledge and acquired a deep understanding of several major sects in Chinese Buddhism—specifically the Vinaya sect (Lüzong). At the age of 18, he was ordained a bodhisattva by Patriarch Dao'an, who was a renowned Buddhist master, and the founding patriarch of Nanshan Vinaya sect. He resided in the Longxing Temple in Kuaiji (present-day Shaoxing in Zhejiang Province). He happened to pass by Yangzhou and was accommodated at the Dayun Temple. He gladly presided over the percept-granting ceremony for Jianzhen, having heard that Jianzhen just turned 18 years old, and that he had a deep understanding of Buddhism. Patriarch Dao'an believed Jianzhen would have a splendid future. In accordance with the ordination system of the Tang Dynasty, samaneras (little monks) should experience a tonsure ceremony and a public ordination ceremony first. When they were 20 years old, they would attend another ordination ceremony to become bhikshus (monks) or bhikshunis

少年鉴真决意出家，随父亲到大云寺拜见智满禅师。《东征传》绘卷，日本真人元开绘。乐敏供图。

The young Jianzhen determined to become a monk accompanying his father to pay a formal visit to Monk Zhiman in Dayun Temple. Panorama of *Voyage to East*, painted by Mahito Genkai. Photo credit: Le Min.

鉴真这样富贵人家的子弟出家，并不是出于生计的考虑，纯粹是对佛教的崇高信仰和坚定决心使然。

鉴真在大云寺随智满禅师学习佛法。他聪明绝顶，又勤奋刻苦，潜心精研佛教经典，加上智满禅师的悉心指导，年纪轻轻便已具备高度佛学修养，特别是对律宗的体悟更深，初具大师的气象。出家四年后，鉴真由道岸禅师授"菩萨戒"。道岸是当时江浙一带的高僧，是南山律宗的开山禅师。他本来常居越州会稽（今浙江绍兴）龙兴寺，于705年路过扬州，住

(nuns). After taking the precept-granting ceremony, they get official permits to be a monk or nun with social status. Before they took a bodhisattva-precept ordination ceremony, they go through the painstaking practice to enhance wisdom, knowledge, and virtue. The precept-granting ceremony for Jianzhen by Dao'an was an exceptional example, which made Jianzhen quickly become a well-loved young monk.

A year later, Jianzhen left the Dayun Temple to be a disciple at monasteries and temples in Luoyang and Chang'an with the recommendation of Dao'an. Initially, he traveled far and studied well in Luoyang for a year. He deeply impressed all the sangha in both

Precept-granting System in Buddhism

Whoever converts to Buddhism should take precepts for enlightenment. Different sects have different interpretations of Buddhism, so they believe in different moral precepts. They can be divided into five precepts, eight precepts, 10 precepts, and perfect precepts (called comprehensive precepts). They can be divided into lesser vehicle precepts, great vehicle precepts, precepts for lay people, precepts for bhikshus (monks) or bhikshunis (nuns). Samanera (little monk) precepts are of low grade, and which are taken by novices under the age of 20. There are 10 precepts that little monks (novices)

拜见智满禅师。《东征传》绘卷。
Visit to Buddhist Monk Zhiman. Panorama
of *Voyage to East*.

鉴真在大云寺剃度出家。《东征传》绘卷。
Jianzhen being ordained as a monk in Dayun
Temple. Panorama of *Voyage to East*.

宿在大云寺。他得知鉴真学识渊博，佛德高尚，且年岁极轻，刚满18岁，前途不可限量，便乐于为他授菩萨戒。按照唐朝受戒制度，僧尼出家以后，要剃须除发，先受沙弥戒，20岁以后，才能受比丘的律仪戒，取得僧侣资格。此后要经过苦心修炼，具足佛学知识，发菩提心，行菩萨道，方能受菩萨戒。道岸此时便给鉴真破格授菩萨戒，使他迅速成为扬州一位颇受尊敬的青年名僧。

should observe such as not taking lives; not taking what is not given; not losing chastity; not indulging in false speeches; not taking intoxicants; not taking food at inappropriate time; not dancing, singing or playing music or watching entertainment programs; not using perfume, cosmetics, wearing of garlands; not using high chairs or sleeping on luxurious bed; and not accepting gold and silver (money). When novices are at the age of 20, they receive an official ordination ceremony to become bhikshus or bhikshunis. After being ordained, bhikshus or bhikshunis will observe Perfect Precepts or Great Precepts, which means they can now abide by all the required precepts "perfectly well." In the ordination ceremony, the candidate takes an oath to observe complete precepts in the presence of 10 monks known as the "three leaders and seven witnesses." The ordination ceremony must be held at a particular place (precept platform) and in accordance with a specific procedure. Perfect Precepts are the most important for bhikshus or bhikshunis, because only by taking Perfect Precepts they will be fully recognized as a member of sangha—Buddhism monastic community. As for receivers believing in Chinese Buddhism, a sect of Zen Buddhism, they are required to observe bodhisattva precepts. Bhikshus are required to observe over 200 precepts, and bhikshunis, over 300 precepts. In the ordination ceremony, receivers will be burned in the forehead or wrist with burning incense to form three, six, nine or 12 black marks. The more marks, the more pious. All the receivers should not break their oaths. If they do not wish to continue as Buddhists, they can announce in advance not to observe precepts anymore, and give up their Buddhist lives.

佛教受戒制度

凡皈依佛教的人都应受持戒律，以便更好地修行。因不同教派对教义有不同理解，所以产生了不同的戒条，可分为五戒、八戒、十戒、具足戒等，或分为小乘戒、大乘戒、居士戒、比丘戒、比丘尼戒等。等级较低的是沙弥戒，一般授予20岁以下的僧尼。沙弥戒有十个戒条，即不杀生、不偷盗、不行淫、不妄语、不饮酒、不涂饰香鬘、不视听歌舞、不坐高广大床、不非时食、不蓄金银财宝。出家人到20岁时正式开始受比丘戒或比丘尼戒，也称"具足戒"，意为"具备充足的戒条"，或称"大戒"。受戒时必须具足一切条件，如特定的监察僧人（十师）、特定的受戒场所（戒坛）、特定的法会程序等。具足戒是比丘、比丘尼必须受的最重要的戒，受了此戒后才算最正规的佛教徒。信奉大乘佛教的汉地佛教僧尼还须受菩萨戒。具足戒戒条甚多，比丘要守200多戒，比丘尼更多达300多戒。受戒时要用戒香炙烧头额或手腕，炙成三个、六个、九个或12个黑疤，越多表示越虔诚。凡受戒者不许破戒，如果不愿意过出家生活，可以声明舍戒，还俗回家。

the White Horse Temple and Huilin Temple with his rich knowledge and kind attitude. In the spring of year 707, Jianzhen arrived in Chang'an and resided in the Shiji Temple. With the recommendation of Dao'an, Jianzhen became a disciple of Master Hongjing. Master Hongjing was well-versed in both Vinaya sect (Lüzong) and Tiantai sect (Tiantaizong). Master Hongjing and Patriarch Dao'an were both summoned by the Emperor Zhongzong of the Tang Dynasty to become senior monks to hold the precept-granting ceremonies for the imperial court. After rounds of private talks, Hongjing deeply impressed Jianzhen with his profound erudition, and his informative and in-depth debates. Jianzhen was deeply enlightened. Jianzhen also gave Hongjing a deep impression with his excellence at dharmar, his broad horizon, and his insight. Hongjing regarded him as a rare talent of Buddhism. On March 28 (lunar calendar), 708, Jianzhen took the Perfect Precepts at the Shiji Temple. Hongjing, who was 75 years old, presided over the precept-granting ceremony for Jianzhen, who was 21 at that time. Jianzhen became the last among the people ordained by Hongjing.

The two capital cities, Luoyang and Chang'an, were then political, economic and cultural centers of China, where the history of Buddhism can be tracked longer than that in Yangzhou. There were rows of monasteries

　　一年之后，鉴真又由道岸禅师引荐，离开扬州大云寺去洛阳、长安的古寺名刹游学深造。他先在洛阳游学一年，白马寺、慧林寺里的高僧佛徒都对这个渊博、平易的年轻和尚留下深刻印象。鉴真于707年春到达长安，寄住在实际寺。鉴真又经道岸介绍，拜高僧弘景为师。弘景既是律宗名僧，又是天台宗大师，与道岸一起被唐中宗召进朝廷担任授戒师。鉴真与弘景几番交谈，深感弘景大师学问渊博，议论深刻剀切，闻之如醍醐灌顶。弘景也感到鉴真精通律学，眼界开阔，造诣精深，为佛门之稀有奇才，便于708年农历三月二十八日在实际寺给鉴真授了"具足戒"，当时的鉴真年方21岁。此时的弘景已是75岁高龄，年轻的鉴真和尚成为他最后一个授戒的弟子。

　　洛阳、长安两京是当时中国的政治、经济、文化中心，宗教传入也早于扬州。两京佛寺林立，高僧荟萃，论辩激烈，宗教氛围浓郁。鉴真虔敬地游学于两座都城，历访名寺高僧，潜心钻研佛学经典特别是律学教义，26岁回到扬州时已成为一位造诣极高的律学大师。鉴真所学，以律学为主，兼修天台宗、华严宗等派经典。

and temples, where the sangha often heatedly debated in a strong religious atmosphere. Jianzhen with great piety traveled widely in the two capitals, frequently visited famous monasteries and monks, and concentrated on studying Buddhism—especially dharmar verses and doctrines. At the age of 26, when he returned to his hometown Yangzhou, he was already a highly accomplished dharmar master. He was well-versed in doctrines in Tiantai sect (Tiantaizong) and Huayan sect (Huayanzong).

China's feudal economy and culture, and arts, reached their peak level in the "Kaiyuan Era" in which Jianzhen lived. The architecture of Chinese palaces and temples reached a mature level after great developments in the Han Dynasty (206 BC–220 AD), Jin Dynasty (265–420), and Northern and Southern Dynasties (420–589). In Luoyang and Chang'an, there were numerous temples with gorgeous outer appearances and unique styles, which dwarfed the houses for great feudal lords, generals and ministers of the Tang Dynasty. Jianzhen was an architectural expert. Before Jianzhen traveled to the two capital cities, he had presided over the construction of the Longxing Temple and the Kaiyuan Temple in Yangzhou. He never missed any chance to improve his architecture design skills. Jianzhen had a much deeper understanding of Buddhist architecture

鉴真参与建造的小雁塔。Fotoe供图。
The Small Goose Pagoda that Jianzhen took a hand in building. Photo credit: Fotoe.

鉴真所处的"开元盛世"，是中国封建经济和文化、艺术空前发展的高峰时代。中国的宫殿建筑和寺庙建筑，经过汉（前206—公元220）、晋（265—420）、南北朝（420—589）的大规模发展，也已达到成熟时期。洛阳和长安的名刹大寺数不胜数，庄严华丽，风格各异，即使王侯将相的宅邸也相形见绌。鉴真是一名建筑能手，在扬州时就主持修建过龙兴寺和

arts in the two cities. In the autumn of year 708, before he was about to return to Yangzhou, he paid a visit to his mentor Dao'an to bid farewell. Dao'an was busy with the construction of the Small Goose Pagoda in the Jianfu Temple of Chang'an. Knowing that Jianzhen excelled at construction, Dao'an asked Jianzhen to join him. Jianzhen agreed. Throughout the process of constructing the Small Goose Pagoda, Jianzhen worked very hard by observing and studying conscientiously and participating in some of the design, construction, and decoration work, thus accumulating a lot of practical experience. It laid a solid foundation for him to preside over the construction of the Tōshōdai-ji Temple in Japan when Jianzhen was at his later years.

Chang'an was a place where professional doctors and physicians gathered. When Master Hongjing taught

Major Buddhism sects in China

There are many Buddhism sects in China with eight popular sects. They are: (1) Sanlun or Three Sutra sect—also called Dharma-nature sect; (2) Yogacara sect—also called Faxiang sect; (3) Tiantai sect or Lotus sect; (4) Garland sect—also called Huayan sect; (5) Chan sect or Zen; (6) Pure Land sect; (7) Vinaya sect or Lüzong; and (8) Mi sect—also called Esoteric sect.

开元寺，这样的大好学习机会他自然不会放过。鉴真对于佛寺建筑艺术的理解更深入了。708年秋，鉴真打算启程回扬州，去向恩师道岸辞别。道岸当时正忙于建造长安荐福寺的小雁塔，因鉴真精通建筑，便请他协助自己。在整个营造过程中，鉴真不辞辛劳，认真观察和学习，还亲自参加一些设计、施工、装饰工作，积累了很多实际经验。这为他晚年主持修建名闻遐迩的日本唐招提寺打下了深厚的基础。

长安也是名医云集的地方。鉴真在向弘景法师学习"五明医学药典"时，弘景带他到皇宫"太医署"，见到了不少医林高手，得到不少秘传医方，包括珍贵稀有的《唐本草》。鉴真刻苦学习，掌握了中

中国佛教的宗派

中国佛教曾出现过许多派别，流行的主要有八宗。一是三论宗，又名法性宗；二是瑜伽宗，又名法相宗；三是天台宗；四是贤首宗，又名华严宗；五是禅宗；六是净土宗；七是律宗；八是密宗，又名真言宗。这就是通常所说的性、相、台、贤、禅、净、律、密八大宗派。

Jianzhen to learn *Wuming Medicine and Pharmacopoeia*, Hongjing often brought Jianzhen to the "imperial physician department," where Jianzhen met some medical masters and got some rare collected exegesis of recipes, including the priceless *Tang Materia Medica*. Jianzhen studied hard, mastered the principles of medical science and a lot of traditional Chinese medicine prescriptions, accumulated a wealth of medical experience by means of clinical differentiation of lots of syndromes of patients with different diseases eventually becoming a famous monk proficient in medicine.

When Jianzhen studied in Luoyang and Chang'an, he got some general idea about Japan. At the beginning of the Tang Dynasty, Japan regularly dispatched ambassadors and students to China. About 78% of the students were the sangha, most of who went to Luoyang and Chang'an to study Chinese culture, religion, and literature. During his travel and study in the two capital cities, Jianzhen heard of mutual exchange in Buddhism between China and Japan, which gave him a deep impression. One of the legendary stories goes like this: Long ago, there lived a monk named Huisi in China. After his nibbana (blowing out or extinction), he was reborn in Japan and became a prince. The prince believed in Buddhism, spreading the Buddhist precepts among the common people, and contributed to the

医的医理和大量验方，通过对大量患者病症的临床辨证，积累了丰富的医疗经验，最后成为精通医学的高僧名医。

鉴真在洛阳和长安游学还有一个收获，就是对东邻日本有了一定的了解。唐朝初年，日本就经常派遣使臣和留学生来中国访问、学习，留学生总数的78%是僧侣。他们大多居留洛阳和长安，广泛结交，和中国僧侣切磋经典，探讨学问。鉴真在洛阳和长安钻研进修期间听到的有关中日之间佛教交流的传说，给他留下了深刻的印象。鉴真曾听说，在很早以前，中国有一个名叫惠思的和尚，寂化后转生到了日本国，成为王子。王子笃信佛祖，大力推广佛教，普济众生，遂使佛法在日本日渐兴隆。他还听说，日本有一位大臣，善汉诗，信佛教，曾制作袈裟1000件，每件绣有四句偈诗，并托人把袈裟带到唐朝，分赠给当时著名的中国僧侣。鉴真感到日本是佛法可以得到弘扬的"有缘之国"。

鉴真27岁时回到扬州，后主持大明寺，持律授戒，先后主持修造寺庙80余所，并造佛像、修塔宇、广施医药、普济众生，赢得广泛的爱戴与敬仰，号称

gradual prosperity of Buddhism in Japan. Another legendary story goes like this: There lived a minister in Japan. The minister was well-versed in Chinese poetry, and believed in Buddhism. He once sewed 1,000 cassocks, each of which was embroidered with a four-sentence hymn (poem). Then he asked friends to fetch them to China, and sent them to famous Chinese monks in the Tang Dynasty. Jianzhen felt that Buddhist doctrines can be widely promoted in Japan.

By the time Jianzhen returned to Yangzhou, he had become a renowned Buddhist master at the young age of 27 years. Later, he took charge of the Daming Temple and presided over ordination ceremonies. Under his leadership, over 80 temples and monasteries were designed. He gained widespread respect and admiration by setting up Buddha statues, repairing pagodas, giving medicine to the common people generously, and preaching and instilling the Buddhist precepts among the common people. He was granted the title of "Master in Jianghuai (Yangtze-Huaihe) region" because of his "super Buddha nature and exceptional insight." He ordained over 40,000 Buddhists across China, including over 230 famous ones.

大明寺鉴真像。这座塑像是根据唐招提寺中的鉴真塑像复制的。阿南史代摄。
The statue of Jianzhen in Daming Temple replicated based on the statue of Jianzhen in Tōshōdai-ji Temple. Photo by Virginia Anami.

"道俗归心，独秀无伦"的"江淮化主"。他为之授戒的佛教信徒多达4万余人，遍布全国各地，其中著名的就有230多人。

II

Invited to Sail Eastwards

Buddhism was introduced to Japan by China in around year 552. At that time, Japan was in a transition period from clan tribes to an ancient farming country, and the rulers used Buddhism and Confucianism to meet the demands of promoting social changes. Buddhism and Confucianism became political and ideological pillars for Japan. After Prince Shotoku (574–621) became the regent of Japan in year 593, he decisively implemented the Taika Reform and vigorously promoted Buddhism to enhance imperial power and rectify social chaos. Buddhism greatly developed during Shotoku's regime. In the latter part of his ruling era, there were 46 temples and over 1,300 monks and nuns across Japan.

After the Taika Reform, Japan dispatched envoys to the Tang Dynasty 15 times to absorb Chinese culture. A typical envoy group may comprise an ambassador and his deputies, sailors, doctors, scholars, students, and monks.

2

应邀东渡

佛教大概是在552年从中国传入日本的。当时的日本正处在从氏族部落联合体向古代国家转型时期，

圣德太子坐像。日本奈良法隆寺藏。乐敏供图。
Seated statue of Prince Shyotoku. Photo credit: Le Min.

佛教迎合了统治阶层推动社会变革的需求，与儒学一起成为促进日本古代国家成型的两大政治思想支柱。593年，圣德太子（574—621）开始摄政，面对社会混乱不堪的危局，果断推行"大化革新"，并大力提倡佛教，借以提高皇权。佛教因此在

Japan suffered great losses and costs to sail westwards to China due to limited navigation technology. Shipwrecks took place one after another, and about one quarter of the crew and several ambassadors failed to survive. Undeterred by hardships, the Japanese continued to send more envoy groups to China with strong determination and urgent desire to learn Chinese culture.

During Japan's Nara period, the Mikado (Emperor of Japan) followed the example of China in constructing temples and monasteries, make gigantic Buddha statues, and to establish Buddhism as the State religion. Due to social disruption and heavier enslavement, farmers and other lay people often became monks simply to avoid paying taxes. For the lack of competent masters to grant precepts, it was difficult to find normal precept-granting ceremonies. Some people burned incense in front of Buddha statues and claimed to take precepts themselves. They did not know the Buddhist precepts and failed to abide by them. The disorder and lack of discipline among the monks and nuns resulted in a variety of social chaos at the beginning of the 8th century.

Senior monks by virtue of the court's power did whatever they wanted to do. Some senior monks neither chanted sutras nor resided in monasteries or temples, while even worse others pursued personal profits and women as their wives. The breakdown of Buddhism

河南洛阳周公庙日本遣隋使遣唐使访都碑。Fotoe供图。
The stone-tablet pavilion of Japanese Imperial
embassies to China in Zhougong Temple, Luoyang,
Henan. Photo credit: Fotoe.

日本得到很大发展，到圣德太子统治后期，全日本已有寺庙46座，僧尼1300余人。

大化革新后，日本出现了一个吸收中国文化的更大的热潮，先后派出15次遣唐使前来中国。在到中国学习的日本留学人员中，有许多是前来求法的僧侣。在航海技术有限、难以预料成败生死的年代，这种渡海行动危险极大、牺牲惨重。海难频频发生，约有四分之一的船上人员及数位大使未能生还。日本民族以

Envoys to Tang China

Envoys (Imperial embassies) to the Tang Dynasty refer to a group of people that the Japanese imperial court official dispatched to China during the Tang Dynasty (7th–9th centuries). Its predecessor was "envoys to the Sui Dynasty." In the ruling of Shotoku, he was keen on reforms. To directly draw on Chinese advanced culture, he sent an envoy group to Chinese Sui Dynasty in year 600 led by Ono no Imoko. He again sent three more envoy groups to China in years 607, 608, and 614. After the founding of the Tang Dynasty, the Japanese court continued this policy. In over 260 years (630–895), the Japanese court dispatched envoys to China for 19 times, among which three were suspended and one failed to China. Only 15 times, envoys to the Tang Dynasty reached China. A typical envoy group comprised an ambassador and his deputies, clerical assistants, doctors, translators, painters, musicians, students, and monks. The scale of envoy groups was initially small, but it became larger later. A typical envoy group was made of about 500 people, who took four ships. In year 838, the Japanese court dispatched the 18th envoy group, which had the maximum number of envoys, totaling 651. Initially, those envoy groups sailed north, then crossed the China East Sea, and finally directly landed on the ports along the Yangtze River. After reaching the Tang regime, they typically traveled and studied in Chang'an or other places for about one year.

遣唐使

遣唐使指为学习中国文化，日本朝廷自7世纪至9世纪向唐朝中国派遣的官方使团。遣唐使的前身是遣隋使。圣德太子摄政后，锐意改革，为了直接吸取中国的先进文化，于600年派出小野妹子率领的使团渡海出使隋朝。后又派三次遣隋使（607、608、614）。唐朝建立后，日本朝廷继续这一政策，从630—895年的260多年间，共任命了19次遣唐使，因故中止三次，实际成行16次，真正到达中国的只有15次。使团除有大使、副使等官员，文书、医生、翻译、画师、乐师等各类随员外，还带留学生和留学僧同行。遣唐使团的规模，初期较小，中、后期比较庞大，一般约500余人，分乘四艘海船，人数最多的是838年的第18次，达651人。初期取北路航线，后横渡东海，直接至长江口岸登陆。遣唐使臣在长安和内地一般要逗留一年左右，到处参观访问、考察学习。

canon, disorder in monasteries and temples, and the situation of farmers seeking to avoid paying taxes—all these problems became more serious, which left the Japanese court and devout Buddhists truly worried and forced them to find solutions to these problems.

In year 684, the Japanese court set up the Supreme Buddhist Administrative Organ, and appointed monk officials of three different ranks among clergy (Sojo—highest rank, Sozu—second highest rank, and Risshi—third highest rank) to be in charge of daily operations to regulate the discipline of the sangha—Buddhist monastic community. In year 720, the court passed a decree that a system of "official administration of the sangha" should be carried out, in which if a member of the sangha wanted to be recognized as a monk, he should get an official permit. Otherwise, they lack official status. This decree did not prevent farmers from avoiding taxes and doing labor, nor did it prevent senior monks from leading corrupt and degenerated lives. The Nara government came to realize that the reform needed to be carried out based on spreading internal doctrines and rules of the Buddhism. Only by helping Buddhists enhance self-discipline to abide by Buddhist stipulations, can they stop doing illegal acts. A sound system of taking precepts among monks and nuns was also introduced to Japan, after an envoy group (delegation) to the Tang Dynasty of China returned

坚强决心和对中国文化的急切向往，前仆后继地进行这项伟大行动。

日本奈良时期，天皇仿效中国，建筑寺院、营造大佛，佛教被推崇为国教。但由于社会混乱、奴役加重，农民不堪剥削，纷纷出家，将寺院作为避难所。由于日本授戒师缺乏，难以举行正规的授戒仪式，许多并不信奉佛教的人为逃避课役，便在佛前烧香秉烛，自誓受戒。到8世纪初，日本佛教界僧徒冒滥、放任自流、僧纪不正，陷入一片混乱。

另一方面，上层僧侣凭借着朝廷的威势，为所欲为，有的甚至逐渐发展为不念佛经，不住寺院，专营私利，甚至专养妻室。教规废弛、寺院混乱、纳税服役百姓减少的状况，已经到了十分严重的地步，使日本朝廷和佛教高层颇为焦虑，曾用各种办法对寺院和僧侣进行整顿。

684年，朝廷设立最高佛教行政机关，任命僧正、僧都、律师三级僧官，具体管理僧侣事务，整肃僧侣的风纪。720年，为防止农民剃度，宣布实行"僧尼公验"制，规定每一个僧侣都必须持有朝廷发给的凭证，不持凭证者为非法僧尼。但这些措施仍然无法制

to Japan.

The Nara court felt that this approach can play the dual role of restraining the number of the sangha from increasing quickly and preventing the sangha from violating the society. By following this approach, the sangha will learn more knowledge and the court ruling will be consolidated in a more effective way. The court sent Prince Toneri to turn to the celebrated Master Ryuson, who was the abbot of the Gango-ji Temple, for advice. Ryuson said, "The disorder in the Buddhism in Japan was due to a lack of public ceremonies to take precepts. Only after novices took the Perfect Precepts, they can be considered fully ordained. Otherwise, they lack official status." "How to grant the precepts?" asked the prince. "According to the stipulations of Buddhism, a novice can only be officially ordained as a Buddhist monk in the presence of three senior monks and a minimum of seven witnessing monks. There were no celebrated Vinaya masters or qualified official precept-granting masters in Japan." Ryuson proposed that monks should be sent to China to invite Chinese Vinaya masters to Japan to set up altars to disseminate precepts. He recommended two young but promising monks to the court. One was Yoei, and the other, Fusho. Master Ryuson believed these two monks will fulfill the task. Yoei and Fusho were approved at once by the court. Before their departure,

止农民逃避捐税和劳役的行动，也难以制止上层僧侣的腐化堕落。奈良朝廷逐渐认识到，必须以佛教本身的教理教规为立足点，从内部加以整肃，提高僧众遵守教规的自觉，才能杜绝违法行为。此时，唐朝佛教界推行戒律和授戒制度的情况通过遣唐使传到了日本。

奈良朝廷觉得，这种做法既可以控制僧侣人数的盲目增多，又可以抑止僧侣的违法行为，并借以提高僧侣的学问，更有效地为巩固王朝的江山。天皇于是派舍人亲王向元兴寺德高望重的隆尊法师讨教。隆尊说："日本佛教的混乱，都是'私度'出家为僧造成的。比丘和比丘尼必须受具足戒，否则就不能算是真正的僧侣。""那么应该如何受具足戒呢？""受戒的时候，戒坛上要有'三师七证'。然而，日本目前没有精通律学的高僧，没有正规的授戒大师。"隆尊法师于是建议，派人到中国延请精通律学的高僧，邀请他们到日本设坛授戒，传播戒律。他向朝廷推荐了两名年轻有为的僧侣来完成这项使命，分别是大安寺的荣睿和元福寺的普照，很快便获得了朝廷的批准。两名青年僧侣临行前，隆尊法师嘱咐他们，入唐后一

Master Ryuson told them to study hard and to remember the mission of inviting famous Chinese monks to Japan and returning to Japan 10 years late by taking the boat of the 10th delegation to the Tang Dynasty. As a dry land of Buddhism at that time, Japan was eager to find proper spiritual guides among Chinese masters to preach and instill Buddhist precepts among the Japanese.

The two young Japanese monks, Yoei and Fusho, traveled to China in the spring of year 733 together with the ninth envoy group to the Tang Dynasty by sea. They were accompanied by two student-monks—Genrō and Gembō. They traveled between Luoyang and Chang'an, learning precepts and paying visits to famous Chinese

Three senior monks and minimum of seven witnessing monks

Chinese Vinaya sect implemented a strict system of receiving precepts. Only after novices took the Perfect Precepts, they can be considered fully ordained. Otherwise, they lack official status. Moreover, a novice can only be officially ordained as a Buddhist monk in the presence of three senior monks (precept-granting masters) and a minimum of seven witnessing monks. The higher reputation the 10 monks had, the more knowledge the receiver mastered.

定潜心求学，聘请高僧，在十年后有遣唐使船再去中国时一同返回。此时的日本佛教界正如一块干旱的土地，渴望中国的高僧带来传播戒律的沛然好雨。

733年春天，两位肩负特殊使命的青年僧人荣睿和普照随第九次遣唐使船到达中国，随行的还有玄朗、玄法两位僧人。他们往来于洛阳和长安之间，一边学习戒律，一边拜谒名僧，邀请他们东渡日本。有一件比较有意义的事是，洛阳大福先寺的定宾律师为他们四人授具足戒，使他们成为正式的僧人，并真正见识了唐朝严格的"三师七证"授戒制度。他们虽然成功

三师七证

律宗推行的授戒制度严格规定，每个僧侣要取得合法的地位，都必须接受名师的授戒。举行授戒仪式时，须有十位名师在场，其中三位是授戒师，七位是临场的证人，即所谓"三师七证"。十位僧侣的名声越大、地位越高，也就表明受戒者的学问越深。

monks to invite them to Japan. There was an interesting story: Patriarch Dingbin ordained those four Japanese monks to take Perfect Precepts, thus making them monks with official status and giving them the chance to experience the strict precept-granting system of "three senior monks (precept-granting masters) and a minimum of seven witnessing monks present" in person. Eventhough they succeeded in inviting Patriarch Daoxuan (Dōsen) at the Grand Fuxian Temple to spread Vinaya doctrines in Japan, the patriarch failed to grant precepts at the altar (formal admonition platform) because his moral prestige was not so high. The disorder still existed in the Japanese Buddhist community with the mission of rectifying the worsening situation ending up in failure. It became a top priority to invite another master well versed in Vinaya and had great virtue to Japan. Yoei and Fusho visited several Vinaya masters in Chang'an and asked them to promote Buddhism in Japan, and none of those masters were willing to accept their requests. It was difficult to carry out the exchanges between China and Japan because sailing to Japan may come across frequent bad weather. Ruthless waves made lots of envoys lose their lives. Once the ship sailed east, people in it begin a journey of hardships and adventure.

Time flies! Yoei and Fusho lived in China for almost 10 years. They probably leave China without fulfilling

地邀请了大福先寺的道璇律师赴日本传扬佛法，但是，由于其德望不够，道璇没有能够登坛授戒，因此还没有打开整顿戒律的局面，日本佛教界的混乱状况也没有多大改观。所以再聘请一位精通律学的大德高僧去日本已成当务之急。荣睿、普照也曾拜访过长安的几位颇孚众望的律学大师，向他们吐露过想请他们去日本弘扬佛法的愿望，但没有一人愿意甘冒生死，远渡重洋。中日之间的交流、交往可以比作征战，因无情风涛葬身海底者数不胜数，渡海者登舟解缆之时，便是将自己交给了九死一生的命运之始。

荣睿、普照等在中国空忙了这么多年，转眼十年之期就要到了。风闻第十次遣唐使团就要来华的消息，二人自然焦急万分。正在此时，与他们交往甚密的大安国寺僧人道航刚刚游学归来，闻知此事，说："既然在长安找不到有缘之人，何不去扬州找我的师父鉴真大和尚助一臂之力呢？""你是说'江淮独秀'的鉴真大师吗？"荣睿和普照眼前一亮，当即决定前往扬州拜见鉴真。

按照唐朝法律规定，任何人未经政府批准均不得私自出国。为了实现高僧东渡日本的计划，道航思

their mission of bringing a qualified master to Japan. Hearing the news that the Japanese court will dispatch a 10th delegation to China, they became extremely anxious. They met one of their Chinese friends, Monk Daohang at the Grand Anguo Temple, who returned to Chang'an after traveling and studying outside the capital. Daohang said to them, "Since you cannot find a qualified candidate, why not go and find my mentor Jianzhen in Yangzhou?" Daohang also told them that his mentor Jianzhen was renowned for his understanding of the precepts. "Are you referring to Master Jianzhen, having a title of 'Unqiue Excellence in Jianghuai region'?" Excited at getting Daohang's recommendation, Yoei and Fusho decided to go to Yangzhou to meet Jianzhen.

Traveling overseas without the imperial court's permission was not allowed as per the Tang Dynasty legal system. To find solutions to help Master Jianzhen and his disciples travel to Japan, Daohang pondered over and over again and thought it necessary to seek special assistance from the imperial court or a high-ranking official. He decided to turn to Li Linzong for help. Daohang resided in the home of Li Linzong and received regular offerings from him. Li Linzong was a brother of Prime Minister Li Linfu. Although the Prime Minister was not well reputed, he had the necessary political connections to help Yoei and Fusho. Li Linfu advised, "You

忖再三，觉得还是得走高官的门路，就想起了供养自己为家僧的当朝宰相李林甫的弟弟李林宗。荣睿、普照通过李林宗见到了宰相李林甫，这位被评为"性狡狯、口蜜腹剑"的人物对几位日僧倒很愿意帮忙。他建议说："你们表面上只说到天台山去进香，因陆路不便，改走海道。遇到顺风，就直航日本，假如逆风，飘回大陆，你们有前往天台山的公文可以证明。"接着，他令李林宗给他的侄儿、扬州仓曹参军李凑写了一封既像介绍信又像命令的书信："造大船，备粮遣送。"李林甫是著名的奸相，这回倒做了一次热心人，帮了大忙。一切就绪后，道航、荣睿、普照、玄朗，愿意一同去日本的僧人澄观、德清，加上高丽僧人如海，七人结伴南下扬州。

他们先去大明寺拜见了鉴真大师。当时鉴真已有55岁，但骨骼壮实，身材魁梧，颚骨线条硬朗，显示出坚强意志。荣睿、普照介绍了日本佛教界的混乱状况，表达了大旱之中望云霓的迫切心愿，恳求鉴真帮助邀请名僧东渡弘法、整顿戒律。鉴真当即答应帮助物色东渡人选。

第二天早晨，鉴真将大明寺、龙兴寺、禅智寺、

can use the pretext of offering incense in Mount Tiantai. You go there by sea instead of by road, claiming the latter was inconvenient. If you can sail before the wind, you just sail directly to Japan. If you sail down the wind, you just sail back to China. I will ask someone to present an official certificate for you to worship at the Mount Tiantai." He immediately asked his brother to write a letter to his nephew Li Cou, an administrator in charge of Granary Section in Yangzhou: "Build a big ship and prepare enough food." Li Linfu was a wicked minister, but he did a good deed this time. With everything ready, Daohang, Yoei, Fusho, Genrō, Chengguan and Deqing (another two monks who wanted to go to Japan together), and Ruhai (a Korean monk) sailed southwards to Yangzhou.

Yoei and Fusho visited Jianzhen at the Daming Temple in Yangzhou initially. Albeit 55 years old at that time, Jianzhen was in good physical condition. Yoei and Fusho told him about their wish to bring the Buddhist precepts to Japan after they introduced the disorder in Japanese Buddhist community. Sensing the imperative need of the hour for Japanese Buddhists, Jianzhen agreed to select suitable candidates for Japan.

The next morning, Jianzhen got together over 30 disciples from the Daming Temple, Longxing Temple, Chanzhi Temple, and Jiji Temple, summoning to them solemnly: "The land in Japan, as our neighboring country

既济寺的30多名弟子召来，庄严郑重地说："东土日本，乃中国一衣带水的邻邦，佛法昌明之地，信徒日众，佛缘甚笃。日本高僧曾经表示对中国和中国佛教界的认同、崇敬之心，他们认为'山川异域，风月同天'，中日两国都是佛门乐土。然而近年来日本佛门纲纪不修，佛戒废弛，毫无向佛之心之凡众宣称自戒，混入空门以躲避徭役捐税，更有不逞之徒枉披袈裟，贪赃枉法，败坏纲纪，乃至公然娶妻生子。日本皇家设僧都僧正管拘，成效不彰。日本佛缘尚浅，尤其缺乏精通律学之大德高僧为僧众授戒，致使鱼龙混杂、泥沙俱下，情势颇堪忧虑。今日本佛界恳请中土佛门修行圆满比丘东渡传扬佛法、整顿佛门，为信众授戒。此乃弘佛大德之事，诸位弟子谁愿前往东土？"

鉴真问毕，室内鸦雀无声，众弟子面面相觑，久不回答。沉默了好一会儿，鉴真将目光移向弟子祥彦。祥彦道："日本国大海相隔，沧海淼漫，凶吉难测，倘遭厄难，岂不了结此生？人生宝贵，死难复生，而况我们这些人进修未备，道果未克，因此之故，大家缄默不答。"其他弟子也纷纷附和。听了这

in the east, is a place where Buddhism used to prosper and there were lots of Buddhists with deep Buddha nature. Japanese monks recognize and show respect to Chinese Buddhism and our country. They think that 'though Japan and China are two different countries, they share the same sun and moon.' Both countries should be paradise for Buddhists. In recent years, Buddhist disciplines and precepts in Japan are followed. Many non-Buddhists claimed to be Buddhists all by themselves just to avoid paying taxes and doing too much labor. Still worse, many monks resorted to illegal acts, ignoring the discipline, and even marrying and raising babies. The royal Japanese court set up an administrative department, but it failed to address these problems. For the time being, the Buddha spirit was still not deeply rooted in Japan. There were no qualified Vinaya masters to grant precepts in Japan. The situation in Japan is quite worthy of concern. The Japanese Buddhist community asked us to help it by inviting famous monks with good virtue to disseminate Buddhist doctrines, rectify Buddhism and make the Buddhist precepts permeated in the entire Japanese Buddhist community. Is any of you willing to shoulder the important task of going to Japan to promote the precepts?"

After Jianzhen completed speaking, his disciples looked at each other with none of them speaking up. There

张家港鉴真东渡纪念馆藏东渡船模型。Fotoe供图。
The models of ship sailing to Japan in Jianzhen Memorial Hall, Zhangjiagang. Photo credit: Fotoe.

was total silence in the room. After keeping silent after a while, Jianzhen fixed his eyes on Xiangyan, one of his favorite disciples. Xiangyan said, "The vast sea separates Japan from China. One should come across expected or unexpected hardships and misfortunes in the vast sea. We should be lucky to even reach Japan alive. It is more likely we may go down with our ships and lose our lives. Life is precious as everyone has only one life. We are also still far from being a grand master. For these reasons, we all kept silent." Other disciples echoed with a nod. On hearing these remarks, Jianzhen did not lose temper. He said firmly and decisively, "It is worth sacrificing our lives to pass Buddha's teachings to the Japanese! As none of you is brave enough, I will go to Japan to spread the Buddha's precepts." The 55-year-old Jianzhen was determined to go to Japan by sea, and this made his disciples ashamed. Xiangyan said promptly, "I will follow you, Master." Then, 30-plus disciples, including Daohang, Daoxing, Situo, and Ruhai, followed the suit. They all expressed willingness to follow Jianzhen to promote the Buddhist teachings and precepts in Japan. Jianzhen designated 21 disciples to start the journey to Japan.

些话，鉴真并未动怒，而是坚决果断地说："是为法事也，何惜身命！诸人不去，我即去耳！"年过半百的鉴真大师毅然要亲自渡海，使30多个弟子一个个倍感羞愧。祥彦随即说："师父若去，祥彦也去。"接着，道航、道兴、思托、如海等30余人也同声表示，愿意陪师父远涉重洋，东渡日本，弘扬佛法。鉴真当即指定其中的21人同行。

III

Five Failures

Making up his mind to cross the ocean eastward towards Japan, Master Jianzhen meticulously consulted Yoei, Fusho, and Daohang. He decided to implement the task of the Jiji Temple. They would request Li Cou, magistrate of Yangzhou, to help build ships, and then prepare the tools, herbal medicines, spices and food for the voyage. Li Cou performed his duties and ensured that shipbuilding work be executed without any interruptions. Raising foodstuffs at Yangzhou—a land flowing with milk and honey—was not difficult. During those times, Chinese were not allowed to travel overseas without the permission of a feudal official. To clear doubts of the feudal official, they claimed that the foodstuffs were a contribution to Guoqing Temple of Mount. All the works were done in a logical sequence. That was year 743 under the reign of Emperor Xuanzong of the Tang Dynasty.

Gyogyo, an old Japanese monk, found Fusho at Daming Temple of Yangzhou. He handed over a collection of

3

五次失败

　　东渡日本的决心既定，鉴真大师和荣睿、普照、道航等人经过周密商议，约定以既济寺为中心分头行动。首先请扬州仓曹李凑出面帮助打造船只，其次准备远行的用具、药物、香火、食品等。这位李凑倒也尽职，亲自过问造船事宜，紧锣密鼓，造船工程在东河口有条不紊地展开。在鱼米之乡的扬州筹办海粮也不是一件难事，只是当时中国人不经官府同意，是不允许出国的。为防官府怀疑，对外都称粮食是送往天台山国清寺做功德的。一切都按部就班地进行。这一年是唐玄宗在位的天宝二年（743）。

　　此时有一位年迈的日本僧人业行到扬州大明寺找到普照，委托他们东渡传法时把他多年来抄写的一大批经卷带到日本去。普照在长安的寺院学习时就和业行和尚打过交道。他虽然身体瘦弱、身材矮小，但想

Buddhist manuscripts and hoped they would take those scriptures to Japan. Fusho came into contact with Gyogyo when studying in Chang'an. Gyogyo, a thin and short monk, was determined to transcribe all the Buddhist scriptures he found at the times of the Tang Dynasty and contribute his part to his motherland. Understanding that the scriptures are numerous, Fusho showed respect to the Japanese monk. They were of great value. Fusho decided not to take them during his voyage to protect the precious scriptures from winds and waves.

When everything was going well, the unexpected happened. Daohang thought that Ruhai, the monk from Korea, was ignorant and incompetent to attend the voyage. Xiangyan persuaded Daohang to take Ruhai with them. Yoei thought it was not a big deal—if Master Jianzhen could realize the voyage, others made no difference. Daohang took a firm stand and said he would quit if Ruhai went with them. Such words were just overheard by Ruhai, who was burnt with anger immediately. He went to the feudal official and reported that Daohang ganged up with sea pirates. During those times, sea pirates were rampant along the China coast. The feudal count had also issued orders to guard against the sea pirates. Ban Jingqian, responsible for curbing the activities of sea pirates, dared not to be careless. He brought Ruhai to trial. He suspected some tricks and put Ruhai in prison pending further

到传到日本的佛经大都错讹、脱漏甚多，不足为信，便立志将在大唐看见的佛经抄录一遍，以对祖国的佛教尽一份力量。普照看着业行抄写的那卷帙浩繁的经卷，陡然生出对这位和尚的敬意。这些经卷太珍贵了，普照等决定这次东渡时先不带去，以免风浪把船打沉，损失掉这份极其独特的珍宝。

正在一切准备工作顺利进行时，发生了一件意外的事情。原来，在荣睿、普照、祥彦、道航和思托等人商议东渡人选时，道航认为从长安同来的高丽僧人如海不学无术，水平太低，出去弘法会有辱师父名声，所以不能让其参加东渡。祥彦劝他：师父东渡传法是众人的事业，多一人就多一份力量。荣睿也认为这不是什么大事，只要鉴真大师能成行，其他人去不去无所谓。但道航的态度特别坚决，甚至说，如海如果去，他自己就不去了。不料此言正好被如海偷听到，他不禁怒火中烧。如海恨死了道航，就跑到扬州官府，易服化名向淮南采访使班景倩告发说："有一个名叫道航的僧人，与海贼勾结，正在城内造船备粮。他们分别藏于既济寺、开元寺、大明寺内。与他们联系的500个海贼，也将潜入扬州城里，展开一场血

punishment. He also sent soldiers to temples and found the new ships and foodstuffs. All the monks were brought to trial except Genrō. Daohang was tormented and still asserted innocence without divulging the voyage issue. The desperate Juanzhen went to Li Cou and presented the official letter from Li Linzong. Ban Jingqian released all monks without Yoei, Fusho, and other Japanese monks. The feudal official held the ships and foodstuffs. Jianzhen sent Daohang to Changan and found Li Linzong and Chao Heng, or Abe no Nakamaro, who was a Japanese student and served as an official in the Tang Dynasty for many years, to help Yoei and Fusho. Jianzhen himself was busy saving Ruhai, who was finally expelled and left the monastic order.

The first attempt fell through!

With great efforts of Jianzhen and under the help of Li Linfu and Chao Heng, the feudal court issued official documents and agreed to release the Japanese monks. Yoei, Fusho, and other Japanese monks were released four months later. Genrō's resolve began to waver and he finally went his own way. Daohang too quit by the reason that he had to take care of his elderly mother. Including Ruhai, totally three gave up the voyage plan. The rest were strong-minded and willing to overcome difficulties and to follow Jianzhen.

Yoei, Fusho, and others made up their mind to prepare

腥的屠杀。"当时中国沿海盗贼蜂起，活动猖獗，朝廷早有诏书，要各地对海盗严加防范。负有重大责任的班景倩听闻此言，自然不敢大意，先审讯告密者如海，看他支支吾吾，说辞有诈，就把他关进狱中，听候发落。同时又急派人马到东河口和有关寺院搜查，果然在东河口找到了新造好的船只，又在大明寺、既济寺找到了大批粮食和物资。班景倩闻报大怒，派出衙役将所有僧人捉拿归案，严加审讯，只有玄朗逃脱。道航受尽折磨和毒打，仍然坚持自己的清白，说自己根本没有和海盗勾结的罪行，并且一口咬定造船是为了向天台山国清寺送功德，没有暴露东渡的秘密。情急之下，鉴真派祥彦找到李凑，拿出李林宗写的公文信件为证，班景倩才释放了所有僧人并归还了物资，但船只和粮食由官府封存。班景倩还以地方官无权处理外国僧侣，须禀告朝廷专门管理外国人员的鸿胪寺后再作处理为由，把荣睿、普照等日本僧人继续羁押在牢中。鉴真一面派刚刚出狱的道航去长安找李林宗和在中国做官已久的日本留学生阿倍仲麻吕（晁衡）帮助营救荣睿、普照，一方面又为减轻对如海的处罚而往来奔走，最后仅仅将其革出教门，令其

for the voyage. Thanks to the high prestige of Master Jianzhen! The fund-raising was successful. They bought a warship from Liu Shilin, who was responsible for ship-building and crushing sea pirates, at a low price. Follow-ers of Jianzhen purchased food, herbal medicines, spices, fresh water, and tools. They employed 18 sailors and a number of handicraftsmen good at architecture, sculpture, drawing, and embroidery considering the requirements of building temples in Japan.

One night of December in year 743, Jianzhen, his fol-lowers, sailors, and handicraftsmen—85 in all—set off by ship. It sailed into the Yangtze River along the Grand Canal and headed to the east with water currents. Soon a hurricane hit them at Langgoupu (present-day Langshan in Nantong, Jiangsu) of the estuary of Yangtze River. The ship was broken and the voyage hindered. They landed on the shoal patch. It was winter, and their ship was crip-pled due to the storm. They lodged themselves in a near-by temple and fixed the ship.

The second attempt failed!

After a month, the ship was repaired. They went on board again resuming the voyage.

Coming across monsoons over the East China Sea when sailing from Yangzhou to Japan was quite common during winters. Jianzhen and his followers encountered the mon-soon soon after they set sail. They had to make a stop on

还俗归乡。

第一次东渡就这样夭折了。

经过鉴真等的艰苦努力和李林甫、阿倍仲麻吕等人的帮助，朝廷正式下达公文，同意放行来中国学习佛法的日本僧人。四个月后，荣睿、普照等人从狱中获释。但玄朗开始动摇，终于与荣睿、普照分道扬镳；经受了牢狱之灾的道航也以家有老母为由，提出不去日本。连同被逐出教门的如海，共有三人离开了东渡的队伍。但剩下来的都是意志坚定的硬汉。鉴真对弟子们说："谁要走就走吧。东渡弘法是大事业，必须有菩萨心、立大志愿，有牺牲一切甚至生命的决心才行。我意已决，就看你们的佛心和意志了。"弟子们都发了宏愿，要跟随鉴真师父排除万难，东渡弘法。

荣睿、普照等人决心已定，就继续筹备东渡之事。靠了鉴真大师的崇高威望，化缘募款得到很大成功，准备了充足的款项。鉴真的东渡团队以80贯正炉钱低价向岭南道采访使刘世鳞买入军用船只一艘。当时正是东南海盗吴令光猖獗、急需军队进剿之时，刘世鳞竟然出售最重要的军用船只，令人不解。后来刘

the Xiayu Island. After a month, they set off under favorable winds. Then the ship was wrecked on a reef nearby Sangshishan Island. Twenty-three were killed including six monks and 17 handicraftsmen. All the materials were lost in sea. The rest landed on a desert island. Jianzhen and his followers pulled through due to their strong will and efforts. A fisherman, who found them, provided fresh water and food, and reported the matter to the feudal official. Five days later, Jianzhen and his followers sailed on the ship sent by the magistrate of Mingzhou and then lodged at Ashoka Temple at Mingzhou (present-day Ningbo in Zhejiang Province).

The third attempt failed!

Jianzhen and his followers received a warm reception at Ashoka Temple. After they recovered, monks, sailors and handicraftsmen—totally 40—were unwilling to go ahead with the dangerous voyage and left. Jianzhen still held to his own conviction.

News of Master Jianzhan living in Ashoka Temple spread out around the east of Zhejiang. Temple administrations within the region invited Jianzhan for Buddhism. Some monks thought Jianzhen was a dignitary and should stay in China. They persuaded Jianzhen to give up the voyage to Japan and requested him to live in Ashoka Temple. Under such circumstances, Jianzhen thought he should go to Japan. To avoid new and

世鳞果然因渎职罪丢了性命。鉴真的弟子们采办了必需的粮食、药品、香料、淡水、佛像等佛门用具和文物书籍，雇了18名水手。鉴真考虑到日本建筑佛寺等方面的需要，还招聘了多名精于建筑、雕镂、刻碑、绘画、刺绣的工匠。

743年十二月的一个月夜，鉴真率弟子、水手、工匠共85人从东河口乘军船出发。军船沿着大运河进入长江，顺流东行，但不久就在靠近长江入海口的狼沟

鉴真第二次东渡准备出发。《东征传》绘卷。
Jianzhen getting ready for his second journey eastwards. Panorama of *Voyage to East*.

鉴真第二次东渡途中，在狼沟浦遇险。《东征传》绘卷。
Jianzhen meeting with a mishap in Langgoupu on his way during the second journey eastwards. Panorama of *Voyage to East*.

unexpected problems from cropping up, he sent two followers to Fuzhou, Fujian, seeking ship and food. He would meet them in Fuzhou on the pretext of visiting Buddhist architectures.

Longxing Temple was the place where Monk Dao'an, teacher of Jianzhen, once lived. The monks there especially hoped Jianzhen would stay there and take priestly vows.

浦（今江苏南通狼山）遇到飓风，船体破损，不能前行。船上人员只得暂时离船，登上浅滩。潮水冲上岸滩，水没到了腰部，鉴真坐在乌草上，其余的人都淹在水中。当时正是隆冬时节，天寒地冻，情景狼狈万状。周围方圆数里又没有人烟，船只一两天也无法修复。众人只得先租船暂时存身，后来又借住在附近的寺庙。

这是鉴真第二次东渡失败。

一个月后，船只修复，大家鼓足勇气，立即重新登船，开始新的航程。

东海上的季风在春夏多为西南风，秋冬多为东北风，在冬季由西南的扬州、明州向东北的日本航行，经常会遇到逆风，风险极大。鉴真一行的船只出海不久，便遇上逆风，不得不在下屿岛停靠下来，等了约一个月才候到顺风，立即又扬帆东行。可是军船刚刚行至桑石山附近，又遭到了大风，船漂来漂去，无法操纵。船砰的一声触到暗礁，损坏严重，最终沉没。船上人员有23人丧生，包括六名僧人、17名工匠。满船的粮食、淡水、经卷、佛像和药材等均散落海底。大家登上一座荒凉的无人小岛，在寒冷、饥饿、干渴

鉴真第三次东渡，在桑石山附近再度触礁。《东征传》绘卷。
Jianzhen's ship running against a rock again near Sangshishan on his third journey eastwards.
Panorama of *Voyage to East*.

When they found Jianzhen still insisting on the voyage to Japan, they were disappointed. After their persuasion failed, they decided to report to the feudal official that two Japanese monks trapped Master Jianzhen to go to Japan. The feudal official at once sent soldiers to arrest the two Japanese monks. Fusho escaped, while Yoei was arrested and sent to Chang'an under escort. Jianzhen was distressed after the news and immediately found friends to save Yoei. After two times of torture, Yoei was unable to walk. The abbot of Longxing Temple bailed him out for medical treatment. A monk died of illness at Longxing Temple. The abbot reported to the magistrate that the Japanese monk had died of illness. So, Yoei came back to Ashoka Temple after disguise.

中度过了三天三夜。鉴真召集弟子们做法事，为牺牲的人们超度亡灵。靠了鉴真崇高宏愿的感召和弟子们的坚忍努力，他们挖野菜、抓鱼蟹、喝雨水，终于渡过了难关。鉴真原谅了弟子们为图生存，破杀戒、捕食鱼蟹的行为，但自己坚守宁舍身命、也不破戒的誓言，只是以野菜、海菜充饥。第四日，风平浪静，他们终于被出海的渔民发现。渔民给他们留下了一些淡水和干粮，回去禀告官府。又过了五天，明州太守派船将鉴真等人救出，安置到明州（今浙江宁波）以东50里处的阿育王寺住下。

第三次东渡也失败了。

鉴真一行受到阿育王寺僧众的盛情款待。众人恢复健康后，僧徒、水手、工匠中有40多人不愿再参加东渡，先后离去。但鉴真东渡的决心依然不变。

鉴真遭遇海难、住到阿育王寺的消息，很快在浙东一带传开了，方圆百里前来请他去宣讲律学、设坛授戒的僧侣与日俱增。有不少僧侣认为，鉴真是一位博学多才的大德高僧，应该留在中国，而不是冒险东渡日本，纷纷劝说他灭了东渡的念头，请他留在阿育王寺。在这种情况下，鉴真感到更应该及早东渡。他

Soon, Jianzhen led over 30 apprentices to Fuzhou to go further eastwards to Japan for preaching about Buddha. When they trekked across the southeast mountainous areas of Zhejiang Province, the unexpected happened! One day, Jianzhen and delegates stayed in Chanlin Temple of Yongjia. Suddenly, a group of officials and soldiers surrounded the temple after they settled in. An official informed that he came to escort Jianzhen to Yangzhou under the orders of Jiangnan Dongdao investigation commissioner. Jianzhen asked if it was under escort. The official answered that he hoped Jianzhen cooperate with his work before returning to Yangzhou. This way, Jianzhen was sent to Yangzhou under the strict surveillance of a large group of soldiers. Fajin, sent to Fuzhou for purchasing a vessel and food, waited for Jianzhen and his delegates for a long time after making everything ready. Later, he got news that Jianzhen was restrained. Under absolute necessity, he had to sell away the vessels and food undergoing hardships—thus reserving a valuable asset.

When Jianzhen returned to Yangzhou, monks living on the banks of Yangtze River and Huaihe River were happy. A group of monks led by Jianzhen's disciple Lingyou welcomed him on the docks. Jianzhen was in low spirits. He asked the chief monk of Longxing Temple that how and who had disclosed information to the feudal official that led to ruining his propagation plan of Buddhism in

宁波阿育王寺。*Fotoe*供图。
The Asoka Temple, Ningbo. Photo credit: Fotoe.

与众弟子商议后，为防节外生枝，决定舍近求远，派两个弟子先期去福州购买船只和粮食，自己随后以巡回朝拜佛迹为名前往福州会合。

　　当地龙兴寺是鉴真的老师道岸主持过的寺庙，那里的僧侣特别希望鉴真留在寺内讲法授戒。他们发现鉴真仍在准备东渡，非常失望，劝说未果，就出了一个下策，到越州府告发说，两个日本留学僧人到扬州诱骗中国大德高僧鉴真，欲渡海前往日本。越州府立

Japan. The chief monk's answer surprised Jianzhen: It was his favorite disciple Lingyou, who had disclosed his plan. When Lingyou and monks of temples in Yangzhou knew that Jianzhen and delegates were trapped in a desert island for nine days and nights, with long-suffering and facing certain death, they worried about Jianzhen and did not expect Jianzhen to take such a risk again. They were determined to appeal to the feudal official and let the official to put off Jianzhen's journey. Jiangnan Dongdao investigation commissioner received a statement from Yangzhou investigation commissioner, and gave an order to the county associated to Yangzhou to investigate the travel tracks of Jianzhen. They escorted Jianzhen to the Chanlin Temple. Knowing the truth, Jianzhen was extremely dissatisfied with Lingyou, and paid no attention to him. Learning that a heavy blow was dealt to his master's cause due to him, Lingyou realized his mistake. The Yangzhou feudal official was afraid that Jianzhen planned another journey eastwards, and stopped Jianzhen in the Chongfu Temple. To show the extent of his regret, Lingyou walked from Longxing Temple to Chongfu Temple and stooped up outside his master's doors from 7 PM to 5 AM—every night. Finally, after 60 days of such behavior, Jianzhen forgave him. Lingyou and another half a dozen monks opposed to Jianzhen's journey eastwards understood Jianzhen's mental realm of great mercy, and completely changed their attitude

刻派人前往捉拿，普照逃脱，荣睿经过了百姓的多方救助无效，依然被逮捕，后又被递解长安。鉴真听说荣睿被捕，心痛不已，连忙派人到荣睿必然经过的杭州找认识的官员斡旋营救。荣睿经过两次逮捕和严刑拷打，因为重伤重病不能行走，由杭州龙兴寺方丈保出就医。正好龙兴寺有一名僧人病故，方丈便禀报杭州太守日本僧人已病故，荣睿则乔装改扮回到阿育王寺。

不久，鉴真率30余名徒弟辞别阿育王寺，开始向福州进发，准备从福州出发，再次东渡赴日本弘法。当他们在浙东南山区艰辛跋涉的时候，又发生了意想不到的事。这一天，鉴真一行疲惫不堪，便到永嘉郡黄岩的禅林寺住下。他们刚刚落脚，寺院就被一队官兵团团围住。带兵的军官声言要见鉴真和尚，说是奉江南东道采访使之命，要护送鉴真返回扬州。鉴真平静地问道："是押送吗？"军官回答道："在回到扬州以前，请大和尚予以配合。"在大队兵卒的严密看管下，鉴真被送回了扬州。鉴真派往福州采购船只、置办粮食用品的法进已经将一切准备停当，但左等右等，一直没有等到鉴真一行。后来他得到师父被拘禁

鉴真第四次东渡，向福州进发途中遇风雪。《东征传》绘卷。
Jianzhen on his way to Fuzhou on his fourth attempt to Japan. Panorama of *Voyage to East*.

and followed Jianzhen.

Yoei and Fusho decided to leave Yangzhou and practice Buddhism in Taiping Temple in Tong'an County to avoid further troubles to Jianzhen and distract the feudal official's focus from Jianzhen.

This was the fourth time that Jianzhen's journey eastwards failed!

Three years passed in a flash! Jianzhen expounded the Buddhism texts and cured the sicknesses of patients every day. It seemed as if he forgot to propagate Buddhism

的消息，万不得已，只好把购得的船只和粮食等费尽千辛万苦卖了出去，保存了一笔珍贵的资金。

鉴真回到扬州，江淮一带的僧侣非常高兴，以他的弟子灵佑为首的众僧侣，早早就在码头上迎候他了。然而鉴真却闷闷不乐。鉴真在龙兴寺问住持和尚，这次出行本来是计划周详、十分秘密的事情，为什么被官府得知，以致坏了东渡弘法的大事。住持的回答让鉴真惊奇万分，原来而惹起这次祸端的竟然是他的高足弟子、佛法修养最高的灵佑。当初，灵佑等扬州各寺僧众得知鉴真在荒岛被困九天九夜，受尽磨难、九死一生，非常担心，就不希望鉴真再冒险东渡。出于对师父的爱护之心，他们决定联名申告官府，由官府出面劝阻。江南东道采访使接到扬州采访使转来的申告书，便下令所属州县追查鉴真踪迹，军队紧急出动，这才演出了禅林寺的一幕。了解事情的真相后，鉴真对灵佑极为不满，从此不再理睬灵佑。灵佑得知了师父心灵所受的沉重打击，才知道自己闯下了大祸。这时候，扬州官府怕鉴真再次东渡，已经将他软禁在崇福寺。为表示悔过，灵佑每夜从龙兴寺赶到崇福寺，在师父的门外从一更（晚上7点到9点）

扬州古运河边留影的游客。塔下运河是鉴真东渡解缆入江之地。Fotoe供图。
Tourists taking photos as a souvenir by the river of Grand Canal, Yangzhou. Under the pagoda is where Jianzhen started his journey eastwards. Photo credit: Fotoe.

in Japan. The Yangzhou feudal official lessened the surveillance on Jianzhen gradually. In the spring of year 748, Yoei and Fusho arrived at Yangzhou again. At this time, Jianzhen was 61 years old, but his great goal remained. Yoei and Fusho said pressingly that they felt worried because their invitation compromised Jianzhen. Jianzhen said firmly that he never changed his mind about going eastwards to propagate Buddhism. He gathered disciples in Chongfu Temple to discuss the issue. They thought they should build ship themselves instead of waiting for the ship to be sent by Japanese imperial embassies. As the money was sufficiently acquired by Fajin, Jianzhen determined to build the ship

站到五更（清晨3点到5点）。就这样一连站了60天，最后才得到师父的谅解。到了这个时刻，灵佑和另外五六个曾反对鉴真渡海的僧人完全理解了师父大慈大悲的精神境界，彻底转变态度，表示愿随鉴真东渡弘法。鉴真认为，灵佑将是继自己之后江淮地区最重要的律学大师，肩上责任重大，就没有同意。荣睿、普照为避免给鉴真增添麻烦，同时也为打消官府的戒心，决定暂时离开扬州，到同安郡太平寺修行，等待机会。

这是鉴真大师第四次东渡失败。

一晃三年时间过去了。他每日讲经授戒，治病救人，好像已经忘记了东渡传法之事。扬州官府对鉴真的监视也渐渐放松了。748年的春天，荣睿、普照再次来到扬州。鉴真此时已是61岁高龄的老人，壮志却不减当年。荣睿、普照恳切地表示，是自己邀请师父东渡弘法连累了师父，心中不安。鉴真坚定地表示了永不改变的决心，弟子们不必考虑什么心安与不安的问题。他在崇福寺召集众弟子一起商议。大家认为，不能等待日本的遣唐使船只，只有自己造船。幸而法进退船款项很充足，于是鉴真决定马上筹备船只，购买

and purchase food and other necessities immediately for his journey eastwards. The newly purchased ship was very strong and splendid, which enhanced the confidence of Jianzhen and disciples. On June 27 (lunar calendar), 748, Jianzhen and his disciples—totally 35—set off from Yangzhou, starting their fifth journey eastwards.

When the ship sailed across Langshan (Nantong, Jiangsu), they faced fierce winds and swell, and the water appeared like ink, forcing them to take shelter on a small island. They again set sail one month later and met a surge once more at Zhoushan Islands. When they set off for the third time, the wind and waves were even greater, the ship bumped violently, and the compass failed to work. The potable water was used up and they were left in a critical condition. When they were frantic and downhearted, Jianzhen told a story about Indian monks undergoing hardships and tramped over the up hill and down dale to teach Buddhism in China. "If they had not come to China to propagate Buddhism in China, we would be confused and miss our way," he said emotionally, "Japan had predestined relationship with Buddhism, but Buddhism there became lax and there is shortage of Buddhist masters. There is urgent need for us to teach Buddhism. Just like Indian monks propagated Buddhism in China in those days, we also come to propagate Buddhism for Japan." His disciples were greatly encouraged and determined to follow their master.

南通鉴真纪念堂。张恕供图。
The Jianzhen Memorial Hall, Nantong City.

粮食和杂物，准备再次东渡。新购置的这条船很坚固也很气派，增强了鉴真和弟子们东渡成功的信心。经过联络，愿意随师父前往的弟子，加上鉴真本人，组成35人的团队。六月二十七日，鉴真和弟子们由扬州出发，开始了第五次东渡。

船只刚过狼山（在今江苏南通），就遇到狂风巨浪，水黑如墨，只好在一个名为三塔山的小岛避风。

Jianzhen and disciples supported themselves by eating rice and drinking seawater. The ship floated its way south for a long time towards the Hainan Island. They were welcomed by local officials when they got ashore in Zhenzhou (present-day Sanya, Hainan), south of the Hainan Island. They lived in Yamen (government office in feudal China), and taught Buddhism to the monks of Zhenzhou. Jianzhen thought it would be better for monks to teach Buddhism in temples and lodged a claim on a prefecture chief of Zhenzhou to live in a temple. The prefecture chief

"鉴真登岸"群雕, 海南三亚南山大小洞天风景区。自左而右依次为: 荣睿、鉴真、祥彦、思托、普照。Fotoe供图。
A group of statues of "Jianzhen's landing," Sanya, Hainan. From left to right: Yoei, Jianzhen, Xiangyan, Situo, and Fusho. Photo credit: Fotoe.

一个月后再次起航，行至舟山群岛时，又遇大浪。第三次起航时，风浪更大，船只颠簸特别厉害，罗盘也失去了功效，加之淡水用尽，情况十分危急。就在大家苦恼心灰、慌乱不安之时，鉴真给僧众讲起了天竺僧人翻山越岭、备尝艰辛给东土送来佛法的故事。他动情地说：如果没有他们来中国弘法，我们就像这暗夜行舟，不辨方向，愚昧彷徨。而东土日本，也是一个佛缘很深的国家。他们那里佛法废弛，奇缺授戒师，急需我们大唐佛界去传法授戒整顿。像当年天竺僧人来中国弘法一样，我们也是去给日本送去佛法、送去光明。弟子们深受鼓舞和激励，决心跟随师父战胜困难。

鉴真师徒靠吃生米、饮海水度日。船只向南漂流了整整14天，一直漂到海南岛。鉴真一行在海南岛南端的振州（今海南三亚）上岸后，受到当地官员的欢迎，就住在衙门里，为振州僧众讲经授戒。鉴真觉得出家人还是住在寺庙里礼佛念经更为合适，就向振州太守提出另择寺院居住。但太守说振州的寺院大部分年久失修，只有一座大云寺还勉强可以，也须要下大力气修缮。鉴真和弟子们没有合适的立足之地，便住

said the temples in Zhenzhou needed repairs, and only Dayun Temple was suitable though it still required some repair works. Jianzhen and disciples had no other suitable place to stay, so they lived in the Dayun Temple and repaired it themselves. After establishing the Dayun Temple, they set off and continued to finish their painstaking journey eastwards. Jianzhen and disciples donated many articles of worship, figures of Buddha and scriptures—that they originally planned to take to Japan—to Dayun Temple before leaving.

Jianzhen and his entourage travelled northwards under the escort of officials and soldiers, and gave lectures. Forty days later, they arrived in Yazhou (present-day Wenchang, Hainan) and lived in Kaiyuan Temple. Unfortunately,

Kaiyuan Temple

In the 26th year (739) of the Kaiyuan reign of the Tang Dynasty, Emperor Xuanzong (712–756) issued an order to construct one temple in each place where major wars took place and named the temples with the title of Emperor's reign, "Kaiyuan." The Kaiyuan Temple was built at the behest of Emperor Xuanzong to release souls of the soldiers killed in wars from purgatory. It is said that Kaiyuan Temples were located where there were large-scale wars. Jianzhen had lived in more than one Kaiyuan Temples.

了进去，又自己动手，将寺庙修缮一新。大云寺开光后，鉴真师徒就要离开，继续他们坚苦卓绝的东渡之旅了。临行前，鉴真让弟子们将本来准备带到日本去的佛具、佛像、佛经都捐给了大云寺。

鉴真一行在振州太守派出的官兵护送下一路北上，途中讲学授戒，40多日后到达崖州（今海南文昌），住在开元寺。很不幸，一场突如其来的大火将开元寺烧毁。作为建筑专家的鉴真受当地官员邀请，担当了主持了重建开元寺的重任。鉴真亲自绘制设计图、指导施工，诸弟子也都尽心尽力，奋勇争先劳动，直到一座崭新的开元寺在崖州的土地上重新矗立

开元寺

唐开元二十六年（739），唐玄宗下令在全国曾经发生过重大战争的地方，各建造大寺一座，以自己的年号"开元"命名。开元寺是唐玄宗为超度在水、陆战争中死亡战士的亡灵，下令在当地建造的寺院。可以说，哪里发生过残酷的大规模战争，哪里就有开元寺。在本书讲述的故事中，鉴真大师就曾在不止一座开元寺中住过。

a sudden fire destroyed the Kaiyuan Temple. The local officials appointed Jianzhen as an architecture expert to take charge of the Kaiyuan Temple rebuilding work. Jianzhen drew design models and guided the construction works personally, and his disciples too made all-out efforts to construct the temple.

After constructing the temple in Hainan Island, Jianzhen and disciples sailed to Leizhou. They went upstream passing through Luozhou, Xiangzhou, Baizhou, Tengzhou and Wuzhou to Guizhou (present-day Guilin, Guangxi). They stayed for three months in Kaiyuan Temple. Yoei had fallen ill when repairing Dayun Temple in Zhenzhou and was very weak, but he still accompanied the group. Under the influence of moderate and cool climatic conditions in Guilin, Yoei's health improved. Admiring the reputation of Jianzhen reputation, Lu Huan, Nanhai's chief commander and Guangzhou's prefecture chief, invited Jianzhen to propagate Buddhism in Guangzhou. This way ran in the opposite direction with the road to Yangzhou. Jianzhen hesitated by receiving the invitation, and went southwards to Guangzhou. But Yoei's health condition continued to deteriorate again, but improved on the way. Jianzhen treated his sickness carefully and took good care of his disciple too. He expressed determination to promote Buddhism in Japan. Yoei died in Duanzhou (present-day Zhaoqing, Guangdong). Facing death, he told his master, "I meant to help you go eastwards

起来。

在海南岛功德圆满之后，鉴真一行乘船渡海回到大陆，抵达雷州；然后溯西江而上，经过罗州、象州、白州、藤州、梧州，又溯桂江而上，到达桂州（今广西桂林）。他们在那里逗留了三个月，住在开元寺。荣睿在振州修建大云寺的时候就病倒了，身体一直很虚弱，但坚强的他一直坚持着与大队同行。可能是桂州温和清凉的气候的作用，荣睿的健康在这里大有好转。此时鉴真又接到久慕他的名声的南海大都督、广州太守卢焕的邀请，请他到广州弘法讲学。这是一条和返回扬州背道而驰的道路。鉴真犹豫了一下，便接受了邀请，南下转往广州。路上荣睿的病情出现反复，日见加重。鉴真极其细心地医治、照顾这位心爱的异国弟子，再三表示东渡弘法的决心不变，希望以此给荣睿以鼓励和支持，让他坚持下去，战胜病魔，东渡回国。但荣睿终因病情过重，病故于端州（今广东肇庆）。弥留之际，他对鉴真师父说："弟子本想辅佐师父东渡，到日本弘法，但弟子的大限已到，不能追随师父完成这项宏愿，心有不甘哪。如果师父东渡弘法成功，弟子就是葬身大唐，也心无憾

to Japan for propagating Buddhism, but my time has come. I cannot follow you to achieve this ambition. There is some unwillingness in my heart. If you succeed in propagating Buddhism in Japan, I would have no regrets even if I were buried in the land of Tang." Jianzhen cried passionately, he put his hands palm to palm, murmuring, "Namo Amita Buddha." Jianzhen touched Yoei's remains and said sadly, "I intended to leave this hot place shortly and return to Yangzhou from Guilin for the sake of Yoei's health. I accepted the invitation of propagating Buddhism in Guangzhou when I saw Yoei's condition becoming better, and I hoped that we could go to Japan by sea via Guangzhou. I never thought Yoei's health condition will change so quickly. Now it's all over!" Shortly after he said these words, everybody cried. Next day, Jianzhen buried him in a hillside near the Longxing Temple. Fusho spread a handful of earth upon Yoei's grave. Jianzhen, Xiangyan, Situo and others followed. Yoei was buried in the eighth year of Tianbao's reign of Tang Dynasty (749). He was the initiator of the journey eastwards, and was the Jianzhen's bravest right-hand person. His sacrifice came as a huge shock to Jianzhen. It strengthened Jianzhen's will to follow Yoei's steps and accelerated the holy mission of propagating Buddhism in Japan to the grassroots level.

Although Jianzhen and disciples arrived in Guangzhou smoothly, they failed to wait for a ship to Japan. They

日僧荣睿大师纪念碑亭，广东肇庆鼎湖山风景区。Fotoe供图。
The Memorial Pavilion of Japanese Monk Yoei, Zhaoqing, Guangdong. Photo credit: Fotoe.

事。"鉴真眼里留下两行清泪，双手合十，喃喃念道："南无阿弥陀佛！"鉴真抚摸着荣睿体温尚存的遗体，沉痛地说："我为了荣睿的健康，本想早日离开炎热地带，从桂林直接返回扬州。后来看荣睿健康有所恢复，就又接受了邀请，来到广州，希望在广州等来去日本的便船。没有想到荣睿的身体变化得这样迅速。现在，一切都结束了！"鉴真的话刚刚说完，四周就响起了一片哭声。第二天，鉴真等把荣睿埋葬在龙兴寺旁的山坡上。普照撒了第一把土，鉴真、祥彦、思托也一一撒了土。此时是天宝八年（749）岁暮。荣睿是东渡的最初推动者，也是鉴真最坚强、最勇敢的得力助手，他的捐躯给了鉴真十分沉重的打击。然而，这更坚定了鉴真继承荣睿遗志，把东渡日本弘法的神圣使命进行到底的信念。

鉴真一行虽顺利到达广州，但逗留了数月，也没有等到去日本的便船，终于断绝了从广州渡海赴日

had to abandon the idea of going eastwards, and the fifth journey eastwards ended with failure. After discussions, Jianzhen, Fusho, and Situo decided to leave Guangzhou and returned to Yangzhou waiting for next chance.

Fifth failure of Jianzhen's journey eastwards

People came to know that Jianzhen had experienced five failures before his final journey eastwards. They had their own versions. Apart from the arguments mentioned in this book, there is one more argument that combines the second and third failure, and classifies the fourth failure into the third and fourth failures. Another statement says that the second and third failures should be combined, and the fifth failure should be divided into two failures—Jianzhen failed to wait a ship in Guangzhou. Even some people think Jianzhen had undergone seventh journey eastwards after six failures. The pronunciation of "seven" is similar to "death" in Japanese, which is ominous, so it was not adapted by Japanese.

的念头，第五次东渡也告完结。鉴真与普照、思托等人商量，决定离开广州，暂时回到扬州，等待时机成熟，再行东渡。

鉴真五次东渡失败

人们都知道鉴真大师东渡日本经历了五次失败，但具体是哪五次，说法不一。除去本书采纳的说法，有一种说法，将第二、第三次合为第二次，将第四次分为第三、第四次。另有一种说法，将第二、第三次合并，而将第五次分为两次，即将鉴真自桂州去广州等待便船未果也算作一次。还有认为鉴真经历了六次失败的，也就是说鉴真总共七次东渡，只是"七"在日语中与"死"发音相近，不吉利，未被日本人采纳。

IV

The Successful Sail to Japan

On his way back to Yangzhou from Guangzhou, Jianzhen developed eye-related problems due to the long spell of sea voyage and extreme physical exhaustion. He could not stop shedding tears leading to further weakening of his eyesight. Seeing this, Fusho decided to bid farewell to the Great Master and go alone north to Mingzhou Asoka Temple to wait for chances to take a ship to Japan. Deqing, a disciple of Jianzhen, harshly scolded Fusho for giving up the dreams halfway and abandoning the great mission of escorting the Great Master to Japan. There were two reasons for Fusho's departure. He was worried about the Great Master's health. He was unable to see Jianzhen suffer hardships anymore. He did not have enough confidence that Jianzhen would succeed in another attempt to sail eastwards to Japan. The second reason was he was deeply grieved due to Yoei's death. Jianzhen knew that the discouraging events that Fusho had experienced in

4

东渡成功

自广州返回扬州的途中，劳累过度的鉴真患了眼疾，泪流不止，视力迅速减退。普照眼看鉴真经受长年的颠簸，体质日衰，不忍师父晚年再因东渡而遭苦难，决定忍痛离开。他想独自前往明州的阿育王寺，等待回国的便船回国。德清因为普照离开师父，就严厉责备他半途而废，背弃发过的护送师父东渡弘法的宏愿。鉴真深知八年来普照所受的颠沛流离之苦，也理解他失去荣睿后，怕自己不能完成东渡大业而失去信心的苦衷。他责备了德清的鲁莽态度，要他向普照道歉，还让普照不要过于自责。鉴真握住普照的手，说："我自从发愿东渡，已经几次下海，但是天不遂人愿，都失败了。虽然决心未变，可下一次出海东渡也不是朝夕之事。不如我们先回扬州，休整一番，再作打算。普照心意诚恳，坚忍不拔，即使离开我回

China for eight years, coupled with the death of Yoei, had seriously undermined his determination and desire to take Jianzhen to Japan. Jianzhen blamed Deqing for his reckless attitude and told Deqing to apologize to Fusho. He told Fusho not to blame himself too much. The Great Master took Fusho's hand and said, "Eversince I vowed to cross the sea to take the Vinaya to Japan, we have not reached Japan leaving our deepest desire unfulfilled. Though our determinations were unchanged, I do not know if we can set off the next sail at once. Let us return to Yangzhou first, and then take next steps. Your intention is sincere and your will strong. Even if you leave me now, I think you have tried your best and need not feel ashamed." Fusho, who prostrated himself on the ground for a long time, parted with the Great Master with grief.

After Fusho left, the condition of the Great Master's eyes deteriorated quickly. Medicines failed to cure, but damaged his eyes instead. He lost his eyesight completely. He told his disciples, "Even if I am blind, Buddha is in my mind. I can find the light illuminating the darkness." The heavy blow of losing eyesight did not deter his initial wish to take Buddhism to Japan. He continued to lead the monks towards Yangzhou. On the way back, they delivered lectures on the Vinaya, ascended the ordination-platform, administered precepts, and converted the people at many monasteries. They did their best to treat

国，也是尽心尽力，无愧于天地了。"鉴真和长跪不起的普照感情激动地依依惜别。

送别了普照后，鉴真的眼疾急剧恶化，服药多时也不见好转，反而日益加重，不久便双目失明。他向弟子们表示，即使眼睛看不见了，但心中有佛在，就有照亮黑暗的光明。沉重的打击并未改变他东渡的初愿，他继续率领僧众一面向扬州前进，一面在各寺院讲法，并一如既往地应邀授戒、度人，有时还尽心尽力地为病患百姓治疗。沿途百姓、官员和士兵都对鉴真的慈悲心肠和高超医术感恩戴德，称颂不已。

鉴真师徒一行一路北行，到江西虔州（今赣州）境内时，鉴真最亲密的助手祥彦又病倒了。他们一行所乘坐的船只还未出江西境，祥彦已经卧床不起。在虔州的开元寺，祥彦已到弥留之际，依然挂念着师父的健康，再三委托师兄弟们代为照顾师父。荣睿去世时凄惨的一幕又重演了。一天清晨，祥彦勉力起身，端正趺坐，问思托："师父起床没有？"思托说："师父还没有醒来。"祥彦说："我阳寿已尽，就要和师父告别了！"思托告诉了鉴真，鉴真立即起床，令弟子设案焚香，移近祥彦，让他伏在几案上，面向

the patients. Common people, officials, and soldiers paid homage and praised Jianzhen for his kindness and excellent healing skills.

Jianzhen and followers went to the north. When they came to Qianzhou Prefecture (present-day Ganzhou in Jiangxi Province), Jianzhen's disciple and closest assistant Xiangyan was seriously ill. When they were in Jiangxi, Xiangyan was bedridden in the Qianzhou's Kaiyuan Temple. Xiangyan was solicitous about the Master's health until his death. He repeatedly asked other monks to take good care of the Master. Another miserable situation came up after the death of Yoei. One morning, Xiangyan sat upright on the deck. He asked Situo, "Is the Master awake?" Situo answered, "No, not yet." Xiangyan said, "I will die now." Situo brought the Master. The Master burned incense and brought an arm-rest. He made Xiangyan sit facing westwards, supported by the arm-rest and recite the name of Amida Buddha. Xiangyan recited the name once sitting upright. Then he fell silent and spoke no more.

The Great Master was devastated by the death of Xianyang. It was so painful when he recalled the hardships suffered by Xiangyan for over a decade to follow him. Sometimes, he even refused to eat for several days. He said, "What a hard life! Why is the destiny so miserable?" Dating back to a decade, several disciples

西方，口念"南无阿弥陀佛"。祥彦按照鉴真的吩咐，清朗地念了一声："南无阿弥陀佛！"然后就坐化了。

祥彦的去世给鉴真的打击是前所未有的。鉴真想起祥彦十年来追随自己的苦难历程，无限悲痛，竟至几天粒米不进。"一生辛苦，何剧于此！"他仰天长叹。当年从长安洛阳来到扬州敦请鉴真东渡弘法的弟子，只剩下德清、澄观二人了。自始至终紧随他左右

扬州大明寺鉴真纪念堂。由梁思成参照日本唐招提寺的金堂设计，1973年建成。乐敏供图。
The Jianzhen Memorial Hall in Daming Temple, Yangzhou, designed by Liang Sicheng based on the design of the Kondō in Tōshōdai-ji Temple in 1973. Photo credit: Le Min.

left Chang'an and Luoyang to invite him to promote the Buddhism in Japan. Among them, Deqing and Chengguan were still around him. Other disciples, Situo, Fajin, Tanjing, and Minglie, never left the Master. Those disciples were all heartbroken on seeing the sadness and solitariness of the Master.

Jianzhen and his followers first came to Jiangzhou (present-day Jiujiang in Jiangxi Province), and then to Jiangning (present-day Nanjin in Jiangsu Province) in year 751. When the Great Master's disciple Lingyou learned of his arrival, he came a long way from the Qixia Temple to the Waguan Temple to welcome him. Lingyou led the Great Master back to the Qixia Temple, where he stayed for several days. They crossed the river and entered the Jiji Temple, where the scenery was familiar to the Great Master. The first attempts to cross the sea to Japan happened in this region. He recalled the olden days with strong emotion. In year 743, the monks stockpiled food and other necessities in the Jiji Temple, as in several temples, before setting sail to Japan. Ruhai, the Korean monk, informed the local government accusing Jianzhen of leading a group of monks to travel overseas privately. The Governor dispatched soldiers to search the temples and had several monks including Yoei arrested. The Japanese monk later died and was buried in Duanzhou (present-day Zhaoqing in Guangdong Province). The

的弟子还有思托、法进、昙静、明烈等人。几位弟子感到了师父的伤心和孤独无告，一个个心如刀搅。

鉴真和弟子们先到了江州（今江西九江），然后沿长江东下，于751年的秋天到了江宁（今江苏南京）。恰好在江宁栖霞寺住持的灵佑连忙来到瓦官寺迎接师父，并把他接到栖霞寺小住。几日后，灵佑送师父过江，住在既济寺。743年首次东渡时，这里是存放粮食物品的地方；如海告官、东渡事败，荣睿也是在这里被官兵抓获的。如今，荣睿的骨骸永葬端州，东渡的僧人们又回到了起点。鉴真大师触景生情，感慨万千。

次日，扬州城里举行了盛大的庆典，欢迎鉴真大和尚归来。前来迎接的僧俗万众挤满了大街小巷，江中的舟船首尾相接。历尽磨难的鉴真大师，在外漂泊三年，行程万里，天南海北兜了个大圈子后，又回到了故乡，继续在龙兴寺、大明寺、崇福寺等寺庙讲律授戒。所不同的是，当年那个身强体健的高僧，而今已是弯腰弓背、眼窝深陷、双目失明的老人了。

752年七月，日本第十次遣唐使团的船队在明州登陆，随后沿运河北上，前往都城长安。普照此时就

remaining monks, who wished to spread Buddhism in Japan, returned to the starting point again.

The next day, a grand ceremony was held to welcome the Great Master back to Yangzhou. The Yangzhou streets were filled with the Buddhist clergy and common people. The ships that arrived to welcome Jianzhen were crowded on the river. It took Jianzhen countless hardships and three years to leave Yangzhou. After covering thousands of miles, he returned to his homeland and continued to deliver lectures on the Vinaya. He administered the precepts at the Longxing Temple, Daming Temple, and Chongfu Temple. The Great Master once was physically strong, but now he became old and fragile with both eyes blind.

In July 752 (lunar calendar), the 10th envoy group to the Tang Dynasty dispatched by the Japanese imperial court landed in Mingzhou, and sailed north along the Grand Canal to the capital city of Chang'an. At that time, Fusho was awaiting chances in Mingzhou and hurried to reach Chang'an. With the recommendation of Abe no Nakamaro (Chao Heng), he visited Chief Envoy (ambassador) Fujiwara no Ason Kiyokawa, Deputy Envoys Otomo no Sukune Komaro and Kibi no Makibi. He urged them to submit a petition to the Emperor Xuanzong of the Tang Dynasty to allow Master Jianzhen promote Buddhist precepts in Japan. Fujiwara Kiyokawa petitioned the

在明州等待时机，他连忙追到长安，经过阿倍仲麻吕（晁衡）的介绍，面见使团的藤原清河大使、大泮古麻吕副使、吉备真备副使，请他们直接向唐朝朝廷邀请鉴真大师东渡传法。藤原清河大使于是向唐玄宗上奏，邀请鉴真和五位弟子去日本弘法传道。唐玄宗虽然也支持佛教，却是一个崇信道教的皇帝。他不反对日本邀请鉴真等僧侣，可又建议他们带两个道士去日本。这让藤原清河很为难。当时的日本朝野盛行佛教，若带道士回去，天皇必然会怪罪；如果拒绝唐玄宗的好意，又怕皇帝陛下不高兴。为了不使问题复杂化，藤原清河留下四名留学生在唐学习道家经典和方技，等学有所成再去日本弘扬道法。而邀请鉴真之事也就不再正式提起，相当于悄悄撤回奏折。他们在使团内部商定，回国路过扬州时停留数日，私下去同鉴真商议，他若同意，就随遣唐使船一起赴日。这样就把本来是正式经官方批准的鉴真东渡变成了一项鉴真的个人行为，在朝廷没有宣布取消禁止个人私自出海规定的形势下，仍然具有不合法的性质。

753年十月，第十次遣唐使踏上了归途，已经在唐为官多年的阿倍仲麻吕（晁衡）作为唐玄宗任命的回

Abe no Nakamaro

Abe no Nakamaro (Chao Heng, 698–770) was the most popular member of all Japanese embassies to the Tang Dynasty. Abe no Nakamaro was born in Nara Prefecture, Japan. In year 717, when he was 19 years old, he travelled to China to study with the ninth envoy group to the Tang Dynasty. In the journey he met another popular monk Kibi no Makibi—known as Grand Minister Kibi. Early in his stay, Abe no Nakamaro entered the National College (Taixue, a high education college in ancient China). Years later, he passed the civil service examinations and became a presented scholar due to his hard work. He was the only one to become a presented scholar among all the Japanese embassies. He was later given an elevation by high-level posting in the court. He was well versed in poetry and literature, and befriended some of the great poets such as Wang Wei, and Li Bai. Emperor Xuanzong appreciated his gift and granted him a Chinese name "Chao Heng." In year 753 when he was 56, Abe no Nakamaro requested the Emperor's permission to let him go home with the ninth envoy group to the Tang Dynasty. Emperor Xuanzong agreed and appointed him to be an emissary to Japan on behalf of the Tang Dynasty to escort the trip. Due to fierce storms over the sea, the first ship that Fujiwara Kiyokawa and Abe no Nakamaro took was lost. When news about the disaster and Abe no Nakamaro's death reached Northern China, Li Bai wrote a poem for him. In year 755, he went to the Tang capital of Chang'an, and was never able to return to Japan. In year 766, he was appointed by the Emperor Daizong as the Governor-General over the subject protectorate of Annam. In year 770, he died of illness. Abe no Nakamaro was considered a pioneer of Sino-Japanese cultural exchange.

阿倍仲麻吕

日本历次遣唐使团中的留学生中，最著名的就是阿倍仲麻吕（即晁衡，698—770）。阿倍仲麻吕出生于日本奈良县，717年19岁时，作为留学生随第九次遣唐使来到长安，同行的还有后来成了日本右大臣的吉备真备。他很快进入"太学"（中国古代的高等学府），经过数寒窗苦读，以优异成绩考中进士。日本人能顺利通过进士考试的，阿倍仲麻吕是唯一的一个。此后在朝中为官多年。工诗文，与大诗人王维、李白等交好。唐玄宗很赏识他的才华，特地给他取汉名"晁衡"。753年，日本第九次遣唐使归国，56岁的仲麻吕请归，玄宗应允，并任命他为唐朝的使臣，护送日本使臣回国。途中遭遇风暴，藤原清河大使和仲麻吕乘坐的第一船与其他船只失散。消息传到唐朝，李白误以为阿倍仲麻吕海上遭难，作《哭晁卿衡》悼念："日本晁卿辞帝都，征帆一片绕蓬壶。明月不归沉碧海，白云愁色满苍梧。"755年，他历尽艰险，回到长安。766年被唐代宗李豫任命为安南节度使。770年在长安病逝。阿倍仲麻吕被认为是中日文化交流的先驱者。

Emperor to let Jianzhen and five of his disciples go to Japan. The Emperor agreed, but insisted on sending two Taoist masters too, which left Fujiwara Kiyokawa in a dilemma. The Emperor of Japan never favored the Taoists, so if they take Taoist masters to Japan, he may not be pleased. If they allowed only Buddhist masters to Japan, the Emperor Xuanzong would be displeased. To neutralize the situation, Fujiwara Kiyokawa allowed four Japanese students to stay in China and study the Taoist doctrines. Even then, the petition had to be withdrawn confidentially. The delegation decided to devise other means too. They agreed to stay for several days in Yangzhou on the way back to Japan. They would meet Jianzhen in private to know if he favored to take one of the ships of the 10th envoy group to the Tang Dynasty. If he agrees, he and his followers go to Japan with the delegation. Sailing to Japan this way became the individual act of Jianzhen, and such act was illegal as the Tang Dynasty never allowed any individual to cross the sea without permission.

In October 753 (lunar calendar), the 10th envoy group to the Tang Dynasty set sail back home. Abe no Nakamaro, who served as an official for the Tang Dynasty rulers, returned to Japan, as a returning emissary for the Emperor Xuanzong. After the delegation reached Yangzhou, they paid a visit to the Yanguang Temple, where Jianzhen was

访使臣同行。抵达扬州后，他们径直前往参谒当时正在延光寺讲学的鉴真大师。在和藤原德清大使的交谈中，鉴真表示自己东渡之心未改，回到扬州后一直在准备渡海，已经筹集好大批所需物品。藤原清河等人喜出望外，使团副使古麻吕郑重表示："一切听任大和尚自行方便。"他们相约，为避人耳目，先将船开到黄泗浦，同鉴真等人在那里会合后出发。日本遣唐使参拜鉴真之后，风声传了出来，鉴真住过和活动过的大明寺、龙兴寺、崇福寺、延光寺等又被官府监视起来，以防止大和尚再次东渡。离开师父多年的普照

日本遣唐使船准备启航归国。《东征传》绘卷。
Japanese envoy to Tang China getting ready to return home. Panorama of *Voyage to East*.

lecturing about Vinaya doctrines, and informed him that they were still interested in him to take Buddhist precepts to Japan. When talking with Fujiwara Kiyokawa, Jianzhen expressed his desire to visit Japan, mentioning that he and his followers were prepared for another attempt to cross the sea and that they had already acquired the necessities. The Chief Envoy was excited. The Deputy Envoy Otomo Komaro did not say no either, "Go or stay, it is up to the Great Master himself." They promised to meet again at Huangsipu (present-day Suzhou in Jiangsu Province) to keep the plan confidentially. Many Chinese knew of Master Jianzhen's desire to travel to Japan after the Japanese delegation visited him. Monks in the temples, where the Great Master lived or lectured such as the Daming Temple, Longxing Temple, Chongfu Temple, and Yanguan Temple were under watch to derail Jianzhen's plan. Hearing that Jianzhen would go to sail east to Japan, Fusho, who left the Great Master several years ago, hurried to Yangzhou. He was ready for taking one of the 10th envoy ships and escorting the Great Master. By doing so, he cannot only fulfill his longtime mission of inviting Great Masters to promote the Vinaya doctrines and precepts in Japan, but also give solace for the death of Yoei. He was eager to meet the Great Master again to render some help, but considering that the Longxing Temple was heavily guarded, he held back and decided

还是从这条消息中听说了鉴真即将东渡这一喜讯，又一次翻山越岭来到扬州，准备搭乘遣唐使船，护送师父东渡弘法。这既是了却自己毕生的心愿，也是对为鉴真东渡事业献出生命的师兄荣睿的一份交代。急于见到师父的普照想去帮助师父做点渡海的准备工作，但龙兴寺戒备森严，恐怕自己会给师父增添麻烦，就克制住自己的愿望，决定暂时不去。

遣唐使团分三批前往黄泗浦（在今江苏苏州）。普照得知鉴真大师将于十月十九日夜离开扬州的龙兴寺，乘船去黄泗浦，就只身赶到鉴真预定的扬州登舟之地等待师父。当天夜晚，鉴真在岸边为24个赶来送行并请他授戒的沙弥授了戒——这是鉴真大师在自己祖国的最后一次法事。这时，普照走到靠近师父的人群之中，报出自己的名字。幽暗中传来师父亲切的声音："是普照吗？"普照激动万分地走到师父身边，抓住师父那骨节粗大、满是皱纹的手，摸在自己脸上、肩上和胸上，感受到无比的温暖和幸福。他感动得一句话也说不出来，不知不觉间，已经泪流满面了。

鉴真一行共24人，有17名僧侣，其中包括智首等

not to visit at that moment.

The delegation went to Huangsipu (present-day Suzhou in Jiangsu Province) in three batches. Hearing the news, Master Jianzhen planned to leave Yangzhou's Longxing Temple on the evening of October 19 (lunar calendar). Fusho took a ship to Huangsipu alone and waited for the Master. On that evening, when they arrived at the riverside and were about to go aboard, 24 weeping novices came seeking the Great Master to ordain them. This was the last time Master Jianzhen administered precepts in his own country. At that time, Fusho went close to the Great Master, reporting his own name. The Great Master's cordial voice: "Is it Fusho?" Fusho was extremely excited. He held the Master's wrinkled hands with thick joints, and felt very warm and happy with the Master's hands on his face, shoulders, and chest. He was too moved to say anything. All of a sudden, he burst into tears.

There were 23 others including 14 monks and three nuns (Zhishou and other two), as well as several foreign Buddhist priests with Jianzhen, who went to Japan with him. When Jianzhen and followers were on their way back to Yangzhou after the failure of fifth attempt to sail eastwards to Japan, Zhishou came across Jianzhen. Moved by the Master's determination, she resolutely joined the entourage. She passed away in Japan. Compared to

鉴真第六次东渡起航处——经幢亭。Fotoe供图。
Starting place of Jianzhen's sixth journey eastwards—Dharani pillar pavilion. Photo credit: Fotoe.

三名比丘尼，还有几名外国居士。智首是在鉴真大师第五次东渡失败、北返途中，受到他的感召，毅然加入东渡僧团的。她后来在日本圆寂。他们这次准备了大量佛经、佛像、玉器、刺绣、香料、药材等物品东渡，带的东西不如第二、第五次东渡那么多，但其中依然有非常珍贵的物品，比如如来肉舍利3000颗、阿育王寺塔样金铜塔一座、王羲之真迹（行书）一帖、王献之真迹（行书）三帖、玄奘《大唐西域记》。带

the second and fifth attempts, they brought fewer items to Japan. They prepared a lot of Buddhist scriptures, Buddhist statues, jades, embroideries, spices, and medicinal herbs on the sixth attempt. Among them were lots of valuable items that included 3,000 small pieces of relics from the Tathāgata, one bronze statue of Amitābha Tathāgata, an original calligraphy by Wang Xizhi, three pieces of calligraphy by Wang's son (Wang Xianzhi) and one copy of the *Great Tang Records on the Western Regions* by Master Xuanzang (602–664). In all, they brought 84 works of Buddhist scriptures, teachings and texts, totaling over 300 *juan* (rolls).

When they met the Japanese delegation at Huangsipu, they were placed in four ships. Jianzhen as well as 13 monks were initially arranged to take the first ship together with the Chief Envoy Fujiwara Kiyokawa and Abe no Nakamaro. Deputy Envoy Kibi no Makibi and other members of the Sangha took the third ship. Fusho, Gyogyo (the Japanese monk who devoted all his life to copying large amounts of Buddhist scriptures), and Otomo Komaro were on the second ship.

Jianzhen and his entourage suffered setbacks in the voyage again. The Japanese delegation held different views on whether they could bring Jianzhen to Japan safely. The entourage of the Chief Envoy discussed among themselves: "Because Jianzhen and his entourage were placed on the

往日本的佛经、论、疏总计84部、300余卷。

　　他们赶到黄泗浦后，被分别安置在四条船上。按照名单，鉴真与随从僧人14人搭乘清河大使和阿倍仲麻吕乘坐的第一船，副使吉备真备和僧团其他成员搭乘第三船，普照和那位穷毕生精力抄写了大量经卷的业行和尚搭乘副使大泮古麻吕的第二船。

　　但东渡的航程又出了波折。日本使团内部就能否带鉴真到日本去发生了争论。有人提出，鉴真一行都

唐朝高僧玄奘（602—664）著《大唐西域记》书影。张恕供图。
Great Tang Records on the Western Regions written by Xuanzang, the senior monk in the Tang Dynasty. Photo credit: Zhang Shu.

first and third ships, once on sea, these two ships would be driven back onto Chinese shores by the winds. If the Chinese authorities find Jianzhen and his entourage, our mission would be in peril. It will be safer to let Jianzhen and his entourage to disembark." The Chief Envoy ultimately succumbed to the above view to avoid diplomatic disputes. The monks disembarked and stayed ashore, which was unfair to Jianzhen and his followers. It was yet another heavy blow to them.

Later, Deputy Envoy Otomo Komaro secretly invited the Great Master and his followers onto his ship. He decided to hold himself responsible if the plan failed.

The second ship's load was very heavy. The delegation had to arrange Japanese monks, who could speak Chinese to other two ships, while Jianzhen and his followers remained in the second ship. At first, Fusho was arranged to take the first ship, while Gyogyo the second. Gyogyo refused to take the third ship. He insisted on taking the first, which the Chief Envoy took, because this ship was larger and more stable. To meet Gyogyo's requirement, Fusho and Gyogyo changed seats. Fusho was willing to take the second ship, because there he could accompany the Great Master and witness the historic moment of Jianzhen arriving in Japan. Monk Gyogyo insisted on moving his chests full of Buddhist scriptures from the second ship to the first one, which annoyed the sailors. At that moment, Fusho helped

安置在第一和第三船上，万一风向不对，把船漂流到唐土海岸，被官兵发现，就会暴露使团私自带鉴真东渡的秘密，不如将鉴真一行留下再想办法更为稳妥。大使为了避免外交纷争，最终还是向这种意见屈服，让鉴真一行离开了船队。这对鉴真一行来说是极不公平的，也是对他们的又一次沉重的打击。他们茫然地困在黄泗浦的岸上，不知所措。

副使大泮古麻吕在最后时刻搭救了他们。他想出了一个折中办法，把被赶下船的所有东渡者都私自安排在自己的第二船上，准备以个人名义承担责任。

因为古麻吕所在的第二船负载过于沉重，使团就分出几个会中国话的日本僧人到其他船上去，鉴真和护卫他的僧人依然留在第二船。普照分在第一船，业行分在第二船。业行拒绝这样的分配，坚持要到更大、更平稳的第一船也就是大使的"旗舰"上去。普照就和业行对调了乘船的船只铺位，这样既满足了业行的要求，又可以和师父在一起，一起见证师父成功抵达日本的那个历史性时刻。业行又和水手们发生了争执，坚决要求把那些经卷箱子从第二船转移到第一船来。还是普照帮助了这位衰老而固执的业行。船上

the old and stubborn Gyogyo out of trouble. All the people on those two ships were sick of the vexatious trouble caused by Gyogyo. No one understood this old monk but Fusho. In the depth of his heart, Fusho had sympathy and respect for Gyogyo, who cherished those scriptures he transcribed in China and intended to protect them at the cost of his life. Gyogyo must take those scriptures back to Japan. He believed that those transcribed scriptures, for which he devoted all his time, would be extremely important for the development of the Japanese Buddhist community. He believed that many Japanese would read, copy, and enchant these scriptures, thus enhancing the levels of Japanese Buddhism.

Only God knows what happened in the sixth attempt. If the Chief Envoy was determined to execute the plan as scheduled, he would not have driven Jianzhen and his followers out of the first ship. If they did not change seats, Jianzhen would take the first ship with the Chief Envoy instead of the second. Those two ships had two different destinies: first was lost as a result of a disaster, while the second succeeded in arriving in Japan helping Jianzhen fulfill his greatest cause of promoting Vinaya doctrines in Japan.

On the eve of October 15 (lunar calendar), 753, four ships set out together. Looking up at the sky, Abe no Nakamaro, who stayed in the Great Tang Dynasty for several decades,

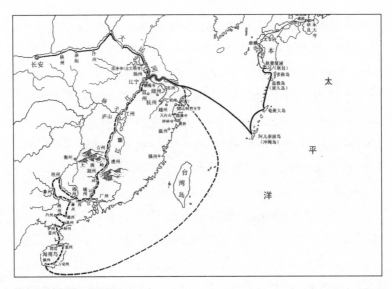

鉴真东渡行迹图。乐敬供图。
Track map of Jianzhen's journey eastwards.

的人都讨厌业行的无理取闹，只有普照真正了解这位
老僧人的真心。业行极其珍视他带来的这些抄录的经
卷，认为那是比他自己的生命更重要的东西，他必须
把经卷平安带到日本。他坚信，这些花费他一生的精
力抄写的经卷对日本的佛教界极其重要，会有很多人
借阅、传抄、诵读，可以提高日本佛学的水平。普照
心中充满了对业行的同情和敬意。

　　如果不是天意，这次换船的变故就难以解释。就
是这个阴差阳错的船只乘坐名单，就是遣唐使团的藤
原大使一时意志不坚，将鉴真赶下第一船，后又将其

enchanted a poem titled *Gazing at the Moon at the Tang Territory* to express his feelings on that evening: "When I gaze far out across the blue-green sea plains, I see the same moon that came up over the hill of Mikasa at Kasuga." When the ships just left the harbor, there was a pheasant flying before the first ship and hitting its bow. The Chief Envoy considered it to be a bad omen and he ordered to stop sailing and lower the anchors, and to set off the next day.

On 16, they set out again. Four ships finally sailed out of the Yangtze River into the East China Sea. Seven days later, they arrived at the Akonaha Island (present-day Okinawa). Because the wind blew north, ships had to stop sailing at the island for over half a month. They continued to sail until the south wind blew. They encountered fierce storms. The first ship struck a reef and was lost soon after it got repaired.

On the afternoon of the 20th of the twelfth lunar month in the 12th year of Tianbao (January 17, 754), the second ship which carried Jianzhen and his followers arrived at the port of Akimeya in Ata district of Satsuma (present-day Kagoshima County), located in southern Kyushu.

Since year 743, when the Great Master first prepared to cross the sea to promote the Vinaya, he made six attempts in 11 years. Though the first five attempts failed, he reached Japan on his sixth attempt when he reached 66 years old. Thirty-six people died in these attempts. Hundreds of clerics and lay-people gave up their efforts.

换到第二船的安排，使鉴真避免了后来第一船的灭顶之灾，成就东渡的伟大事业。

753年十月十五日夜，遣唐使船队的四条船终于一起开航了。就在这个月明星稀之夜，旅居大唐几十年的阿倍仲麻吕作了一首歌《汉土望月》："万里长空碧，举头遥望起乡情。回思春日野，三笠山巅壁月升，恰似今宵一样明。"刚刚驶出港口，一只不知从哪里飞过来的野鸡，一头撞在了藤原大使的第一船船头。藤原大使觉得这是一个凶兆，就下令停船，次日再行。

十六日，船队顺利驶出长江，进入东海，七天后到了阿儿奈波岛（今冲绳岛）。船队因为风向不对，在此停泊了半个多月，直到起了南风，才继续开航。途中又遇暴风雨，第一船触礁，刚刚修好，就在风浪中漂得不知去向。天宝十二年十二月二十日（754年1月17日）下午，鉴真所乘坐的第二船终于战胜风浪，到达九州南部萨国阿多郡的秋妻屋浦（在今鹿儿岛县）。自743年第一次东渡起，经过了整整11年的岁月，五次失败，36人牺牲，数百人退出，已是66岁高龄的鉴真终于第六次东渡成功，踏上了久已向往的日本的国土。

V

Promoting Buddhism in Japan

On January 23, 754, Jianzhen and his followers were warmly welcomed in the Dazaifu (present-day southeast area of Fukuoka in Kyushu). Otomo Komaro could not wait for Fujiwara Kiyokawa and went to Nara—the then capital of Japan—and reported the news of second ship returning safely to the Emperor Shōmu, who had been a monk, and the Empress Kōken. They were overjoyed.

Jianzhen and his followers headed north by sea after leaving Dazaifu. On the first day of the second lunar month, they arrived at Namba (present-day Osaka). Chongdao and other monks, who had arrived Japan earlier, warmly welcomed them. They entered Kawachi Kokufu (present-day Nara Prefecture) two days after they left Namba. Fujiwara no Nakamaro, the grand counsellor (senior official title), welcomed Jianzhen and his followers on behalf of the Japanese court. There were

5

东瀛弘法

　　754年1月23日，鉴真一行由日本僧人延庆引入边防太宰府（今九州福冈东南），受到了热烈欢迎。副使大伴古麻吕来不及等藤原大使，就先赶往京城奈良，将第二船安全回国以及唐土高僧鉴真同船到达日本的情况上奏已经出家为僧的圣武太上皇和孝谦女天皇。太上皇和天皇喜出望外。

　　鉴真等离开太宰府后，继续登船北行，于二月初一到达难波（今大阪府），受到早先到日本的中国僧人崇道等的迎接。两天后离开难波，进入河内国府（今奈良县地）。在河内国府，孝谦天皇最为宠信的大纳言（日本高级官职）藤原仲麻吕代表日本朝廷出面迎接慰问鉴真一行，亲来拜谒的还有日本高僧30多位，包括当年应荣睿、普照之邀赴日传法的道璇律师。鉴真等在河内国府小憩了两天，而后向京城奈良

over 30 Japanese dignitaries including Daoxuan (Dōsen), who carried forward Buddhism in Japan following the invitation of Yoei and Fusho. After a two-day rest at Kawachi Kokufu, Jianzhen and others went to Nara. Kibumi awaited their arrival at the gates of the capital on behalf of Empress Kōken.

After the solemn ceremonial welcome, held by Kibumi, Jianzhen and his followers entered the Todai-ji Temple, where ministers and samurais of the Mikado gave them a warm welcome. The Todai-ji Temple was a large official temple. After Jianzhen settled down there, powerful personalities and dignitaries came to visit him.

Jianzhen sailed to Japan on the second ship. The third ship returned to Japan after a long journey. There was still no news on the first and the fourth ships. When people arrived in Japan by the second and third ships met, they guessed the fate of the other ships.

The Buddhist circle of Japan transformed greatly since Yoei and Fusho went to China and invited dignitaries to Japan and for the successful eastwards sea voyage of Jianzhen. The phenomena that people were ordained by themselves developed wonderfully. The monkhood rites by Jianzhen belonged to the real rituals. As Buddhism exerted more influence on the Japanese imperial family and feudal officials, Jianzhen became popular and prestigious. The Mikado issued imperial decree authorizing Jianzhen to

鉴真抵达日本难波后受到欢迎。《东征传》绘卷。
Jianzhen being welcomed on arrival in Namba, Japan. Panorama of *Voyage to East*.

进发。他们来到奈良城门外时，作为孝谦天皇代表的安宿王已经在那里迎候。

　　隆重的欢迎仪式举行之后，在安宿王的引导下，鉴真一行被引进到东大寺，天皇朝廷的公卿武士和僧人等出迎。东大寺是一所规模宏大的官寺，鉴真入住后，天皇朝廷的显赫人物、皇族中的权贵人物纷纷前来礼拜。

　　鉴真东渡乘坐的是第二船，不久，副使吉备真备的第三船经过漫长的漂流，也回到了日本本土。只有正使清河的第一和第判官布势人主的四船依然没有消

deal with all Buddhism matters and monkhood rites. The Mikado conferred the title of Great Master of Transmission upon Jianzhen, Situo, Fajin, Fusho, Yanqing, Tanjing, Fazai and Yijing. Except Fusho, others were Chinese monks.

On the fifth day of the fourth lunar month, Jianzhen held an unprecedented blessing at Todai-ji Temple and presided over the grand precepts ceremony. Emperor Shōmu came and was initiated into monkhood by Jianzhen. Empress Kōken, the crown prince and officials of all ranks accepted the blessings by Jianzhen. Jianzhen ordained over 400 monks.

After the blessing, the fourth ship returned to Japan. The people's hope on the first ship's safe return was reborn. In year 755, bad news arrived from the Tang Dynasty. Fujiwara Kiyokawa and Abe no Nakamaro died in a shipwreck, while the next year, the good news arrived that they were saved and returned to the capital of Chang'an. The first ship was attacked on the coast of An Nam (present-day Vietnam) and most of them died. Many others died of illness. Only Fujiwara Kiyokawa, Abe no Nakamaro and dozens of others were saved. Abe no Nakamaro went back to his political life in the Tang court. Fujiwara Kiyokawa served an official position in the Tang Dynasty and never returned to Japan. Gyogyo was not among the saved people. This old monk and his handwritten Buddhist scripture probably sank into the ocean or destroyed on the foreign mountains.

日本官员纷纷前往东大寺礼拜。《东征传》绘卷。
Japanese government officials coming to Todai-ji Temple to worship. Panorama of *Voyage to East*.

息。第二船第三船东渡成功的人碰到一起，总是要忧虑牵挂地谈起第一船第四船同渡者的命运。

从荣睿、普照到中国延请高僧来日本传戒，到鉴真东渡成功，这段漫长的时间里，日本佛教界的形势发生了很大变化。那种百姓随便自誓受戒成为沙弥的现象已经大为改观，鉴真的传戒活动基本上都是纯宗教性的了。由于佛教在日本皇家和官员中的影响日益

Jianzhen became the sage monk in Japan. More monks came to Jianzhen seeking blessings, so the Mikado decided to build an Ordination Hall (Kaidan'in) for Jianzhen and his apprentices to promote Buddhism. On the first day of the fifth lunar month in year 754, the Mikado issued an edict that Master Jianzhen would direct the hall construction on the west of the Hall of Vairocana Buddha in Todai-ji Temple. The Kaidan'in was completed in next September. It is still well-preserved within the Todai-ji Temple and became a famous historical site in Japan. To north of the Kaidan'in, there was a small lotus pool. Master Jianzhen built a retreat (Zen-in temple) nearby the pool and lived there. He made 36 spirit tablets for his 36 followers, who died during their eastward sea voyage and chanted sutras to release their souls from purgatory.

Arriving at Japan, Master Jianzhen carried out a strict and standard way of initiation into monkhood, which may cause discontent among monks accustomed to the way of taking priestly vows by themselves. Some higher-up monks still refused to be ordained by the ways of Master Jianzhen at the beginning. Moreover, matters of monks and nuns, monkhood initiation, training and education were under the charge of Daisojo, Sozu and Shōsōzu in accordance with the Sozu and Sōgō-sei system. Mikado gave these rights to Master Jianzhen. Specifically, the Japanese monks were unable to get the ordination diploma, monk's

扩大和加深，高僧鉴真的名声更为显赫，成为皇家和贵族、高官竞相追逐的对象。太上皇委托吉备真备宣读了圣旨：

"大德和尚，远涉沧波，来投此国，诚副朕意，喜慰无喻。朕造此东大寺，经十余年，欲立戒坛，传授戒律，自有此心，日夕不忘。今诸大德远来传戒，冥契朕心。自今以后，授戒传律，一任大和尚。"

这就是说，鉴真可以在日本全权处理佛教授戒传律诸般事宜。很快，天皇又敕授鉴真、思托、法进、普照、延庆、昙静、法载、义净等人"传灯大法师位"。除了普照，其余都是这次随鉴真一道东渡日本的中国高僧。

四月初五，鉴真在东大寺举行了空前的大法会，主持日本佛教界从未有过的盛大授戒仪式。圣武太上皇亲临东大寺，请鉴真授戒。太上皇受戒之后，鉴真也为皇太后、孝谦天皇、皇太子和文武百臣授了菩萨戒。随后，鉴真又为400多名僧众授了戒。

鉴真为皇室授戒后不久，传来了东渡第四船漂流回日本的佳音，大家对正使藤原清河、阿倍仲麻吕和业行等乘坐的第一船的生还又燃起了希望之火。755年

registration and enjoy privileges, if the Todai-ji Temple or its subordinated temples did not ordain them. Such situation was good for the Mikado, but a powerful blow to the old sangha, which controlled the Sōgō-sei system for a long time—both on their prestige and interests. They and the new sangha centered by Jianzhen always had frictions.

The old sangha represented by Kenkyō was opposed to the formal ritual initiated by Jianzhen. They thought the Japanese Buddhism was born with the custom of being ordained by oneself. They were unwilling to implement the formal ritual, wanted to challenge the new sangha, and made an appointment for a debate at Kofuku-ji Temple. To promote Buddhism, Master Jianzhen decided to take up the challenge. He took Fusho, good at the dharma preached by Jianzhen and speaking Japanese language, as his representative. The Kenkyō Party held forth their opinion citing the *Sutra Foretelling the Consequences of Good and Evil Karma*, while Fusho questioned them citing Volume 53 of the *Ontology and Epistemology of the Yogacara School of Mahayana Buddhism*. The Kenkyō Party was confused over how to answer. They were overwhelmed by the thorough knowledge of Jianzhen and truly admired him. They were willing to give up the old customs and accept the formal rituals. After the debate, Jianzhen presented over the ritual of monkhood initiation for the Kenkyō Party—over 80 monks. Fusho boosted reputation and expounded the

从大唐传来了清河和仲麻吕遇难的消息；但到了第二年又传来他们海难遇救、返回长安的喜讯。原来他们的船漂流到安南（越南）海岸，遇到土人的袭击，大部分人丧生，其余不少人也患病而亡，仅有清河、阿倍仲麻吕等十几人得以生还。阿倍仲麻吕继续在唐朝做官，清河也留在大唐做了官，再未回日本。在生还的十几人中并没有业行的名字。这位衰老的僧人和他毕生抄写的珍贵经卷大概都已沉入了茫茫大海，或毁灭在异域的山野了。此是后话。

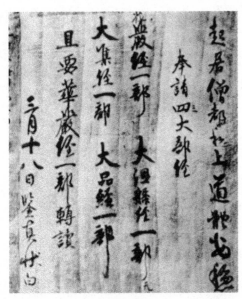

鉴真和尚墨宝，出自日本奈良东大寺正仓院。Fotoe供图。
Calligraphy of Monk Jianzhen, from Shoso-in, the Todai-ji Temple in Nara, Japan. Photo credit: Fotoe.

鉴真成了日本家喻户晓的大唐圣僧。随着前来请求鉴真授戒的僧众与日俱增，天皇决定新建一个正规的戒坛院，专供鉴真师徒传律授戒。754年五月初一，天皇下旨，于东大寺卢舍那佛殿西边兴建戒坛院，并请鉴真大和尚主持建造。这座戒坛院于次年九月竣工，今天还保存在日本奈良东大寺内，成

Buddhist texts at Todai-ji Temple.

In May that year, the Empress Kōken issued an imperial edict appointing Jianzhen as "Daisozu" and Jianzhen's followers as "Dharma." Half a month later, Empress Kōken issued orders that the sacrifices offered to Emperor Shōmu were transferred to Jianzhen and Farong forever. Such decision created great ripples throughout Japan. Farong, a Japanese monk, was good at medical skills and had cured a serious illness for Emperor Shōmu. He enjoyed the kindness of Emperor Shōmu, and even the people of his hometown were free of feudalism. The Japanese court treated Jianzhen as Farong equally and even put Jianzhen's name before Farong, which spoke well for the courteous reception enjoyed by Jianzhen.

The Todai-ji Temple, where Jianzhen lived, was the largest official temple of Japan. It was not the temple for gyrovagues. It was the residency of noble monk and slave holder, which was quiet different from China. In China, monks can roam about and receive accommodation at other temples without time limitation by showing ordination diploma. Yoei, Fusho and other Japanese monks studied in China for years without any expense on accommodation. Jianzhen had sailed eastwards many times with numerous followers and roamed about without any expense. The official temple of Japan held lands and slaves and enjoyed varieties of gifts bestowed by the Mikado and the court

为日本的一大古迹。在戒坛院的北边，有一个不大的池塘，荷花满塘，异常清静，鉴真就在池畔建了一座唐禅院，后来一直居住在此。他特地做了36个牌位，将东渡过程中的36位牺牲者供奉在唐禅院内，天天诵经超度。

鉴真到日本后，推行严格的、规范化的授戒方式，这就必然引起一部分习惯于"自誓受戒"的僧侣的不满。所以开始时，尽管天皇带头受戒，但佛教界的一些高僧仍没有登坛受戒。另外，日本政府原来是通过大僧正、大僧都、少僧都为中心的僧都僧纲制来掌管和处理僧尼有关事务的，授戒、训练和教育事宜也是由僧纲负责处理。如今，这两方面的权力已由天皇下诏划归鉴真，特别是，日本僧侣不经东大寺戒坛院及其所属寺院授戒，就不能取得度牒、僧籍，不能享受免税免役的特权。这对处于统治地位的天皇是大大有利的，对长期把持僧纲的旧教团势力则是个沉重的打击，既影响了他们的威信，又损害了他们的利益。他们与以鉴真为中心的新教团势力之间不可避免地发生了矛盾。

以贤璟为代表的旧僧团反对鉴真的三师七证授戒

on festival days. The official temples were very rich. Such official temples used charity wealth to exploit common people instead of supporting monks and the poor. The Sōniryō (Regulations for monks and nuns) had strict regulations on temples. For example, the temples should not support the foreign monks—even giving accommodation occasionally should not exceed three days, which meant all accommodation charges be paid three days later.

In November 757 (lunar calendar), the court issued an imperial edict under the name of Empress Koken to bestow 100 machi (1 machi=9,917 m^2) of paddy lands on Zen-in of Jianzhen to support the external monks studying Buddhism. Jianzhen had rights to deal with the income coming from paddy lands without any restrictions of Todai-ji Temple. Thanks to the fixed income, the religious activities of Zen-in became active day by day. More monks came to be ordained thus leading the revenue reserves becoming inadequate. There were many poor monks sleeping on the ground during nights. It was not a permanent solution that Zen-in depended on Todai-ji Temple for living. Jianzhen decided to build a Tang-style temple bigger than the original Zen-in. Every monk studying there can enjoy free accommodation. Master Jianzhen went to the court and requested for help. Emperor Shōmu approved the request and bestowed an old residency of a prince on him to build the temple. He committed himself to the temple with rich experience and

的正式仪式。他们认为日本佛教向来就有自誓受戒的惯例，不必执行鉴真的繁琐的仪式。以贤璟为首的旧教团向以鉴真为首的新教团发出挑战书，约定在兴福寺的维摩堂召开辩论会。为弘扬佛法，辨明道理，鉴真决定应战。既精通鉴真的律学又会说日本话的普照代表鉴真一方辩论。贤璟一方引用《占察经》亮出自己的观点，普照则以《瑜珈论·抉择分》五十三卷将对方质问住了。贤璟闭口不答，因为他实在回答不出来了。普照又两次催促他们，贤璟依然没有回答。结果贤璟一方对鉴真的学识渊博佩服得五体投地，纷纷走到鉴真面前，顶礼膜拜，表示愿意放弃旧戒，请大和尚重新授戒。辩论结束之后，鉴真便在东大寺戒坛院为早已等候在那里的众多僧徒授戒。随后，贤璟等80余人也请鉴真重授具足戒，从而化敌为友。普照从此声名大振，就住在东大寺讲经。

　　五月，孝谦天皇又发下诏书，任命鉴真为大僧都，任命鉴真的随行弟子法进等人为律师。半月后，天皇又宣布：将往日用于供奉圣武太上皇的米盐之类物品，永远转供鉴真和法荣二人。这个决定，一时震惊朝野，轰动日本。法荣是一位日本和尚，精通医术，曾为圣武太

design concept over the temple construction. In August 759 (lunar calendar), the construction of new temple was completed and featured with many elites of Chinese temples. Emperor Junnin bestowed the name "Tōshōdai-ji," while Empress Koken wrote the inscribed tablet and issued an imperial edict that every monk or nun can choose the sect until finishing studies at Tōshōdai-ji. To settle expenditures of Tōshōdai-ji, the court bestowed 75 machi of lands on this temple for supporting the monks.

Tōshōdai-ji Temple was the first temple that provided accommodation to external monks in Japan. Monks came in an endless stream throughout the year to this temple from different places. Apart from Buddhism and monkhood initiation, Jianzhen provided them a chance to acquire medical knowledge, architecture and statue skills, Chinese and writing sutras. The temple became a school to learn diversified cultural knowledge of China. Many monks learned there. After learning, they managed to expound the Buddhist texts at other locations. The temple enjoyed a widespread reputation and became a shrine like the Todai-ji Temple, Kofuku-ji Temple and Daian-ji Temple for Japanese monks. The Tōshōdai-ji Temple changed the traditionally closed Buddhism—a tool for the ruling class—into an open and people-oriented religion. It was an important reform in Japanese Buddhism.

Two years after the completion of Tōshōdai-ji Temple,

日本奈良东大寺。张恕摄。
The Todai-ji Temple in Nara, Japan. Photo by Zhang Shu.

上皇医治重病，因此天皇对他十分厚爱，连他出生所在郡的民众也不须再服徭役。朝廷让鉴真大和尚和这位与太上皇关系如此密切的日本和尚平起平坐，共享供奉圣武太上皇的米盐，还将鉴真之名列于法荣之上，足见鉴真所受礼遇之高。

鉴真等人所住的东大寺，是日本规模最大的官寺。日本众多的官寺，实际上不是供养四方僧侣的寺院，而是僧籍贵族、僧籍奴隶主的宅院。这与中国迥然不同。在中国，僧侣可以云游四方，出示僧牒就可以在别的寺院挂单食宿，不限时日。荣睿、普照等日

Messenger Ono Ishime returned to Japan and brought back a rafters supporting tile to Fusho. The tile was a gift to Fusho, but nobody knew who gave it. It was an antique with a deep crack in the middle. Fusho remembered its shape and recalled that he saw it during his life in the Tang Dynasty. It aroused the deepest feelings of Fusho, made him remember his difficult days and dangerous journey with Yoei, as well as the happy days of accompanying Jianzhen.

Todai-ji Temple

The Todai-ji Temple belongs to the Kegon sect of Buddhism and is called Kegon-ji. Emperor Shōmu constructed it in year 728 and the temple has a history of over 1,280 years. As it is located to the east of Nara, capital of Japan, it is known as Todai-ji Temple. The 57 m-wide and 50 m-long Daibutsu Hall of this temple is the world's largest wooden structure. The Daibutsu Hall comprises a 15m bronze statue of the "Cosmic Buddha (Mahavairocana)." The Temple has the Nandaimon Gate, Nigatsu-do Hall, Sangatsu-do Hall and Shoso-in Treasure Repository. The Kongo Rikishi is at the Nandaimon Gate. From the Nigatsu-do Hall, you can overlook the Daibutsu Hall and Nara downtown.

Jianzhen had presented the monkhood initiation ritual there. The temple was inscribed as a World Cultural Heritage Site in 1998 as part of historical sites of the ancient capital of Nara.

本僧人在中国各地学习，从未交过食宿费用；鉴真数次东渡，队伍浩荡，周游各地，也无须花费。日本的官寺有土地、奴隶，年时岁节，天皇和朝廷还有种种颁赐，加上一年四季的各方施舍，收入颇丰。但这些官寺却将这些财富用来放高利贷盘剥广大百姓，而不是用来供养僧侣和救济贫病。而且日本的"僧尼令"

东大寺

东大寺是日本华严宗大本山，又称大华严寺、金光明四天王护国寺。728年由信奉佛教的圣武天皇建立，至今已有1280多年历史。因为建在首都平城京（今奈良）以东，所以被称作东大寺。东大寺大佛殿，正面宽度57米，深50米，为世界最大的木造建筑。大佛殿内，放置着高15米以上的卢舍那佛像。东大寺院内还有南大门、二月堂、三月堂、正仓院等。南大门有很著名的双体金刚力士像。二月堂能够俯视大佛殿和眺望奈良市区。

鉴真和尚曾在这里设坛授戒。1998年，东大寺作为古都奈良的历史遗迹的组成部分被列为世界文化遗产。

He decided to put it in an appropriate place. It was installed on the ridge of the Kondō Hall of Tōshōdai-ji Temple. Fusho stared at it for a long time whenever he went there.

The ruling class utilized the Japanese Buddhism as a bureaucratic tool. When Jianzhen arrived in Japan, the rituals conducted by him controlled the disorderly situation in the private monkhood initiation and eased the sharp increase of monks. He gained the Mikado support. His thinking of bringing spiritual consolation to those suffering by Buddhism and regarding the common people as the objects for promoting Buddhism was quiet different from the Mikado's idea of controlling people and consolidating political power. The old guard of the court became more indifferent to Master Jianzhen. After the death of Emperor Shōmu, with Empress Koken handing over the crown to Emperor Junnin, Master Jianzhen lost the powerful supports. The minority old guard took the chance to mislead Emperor Junnin and wanted to retake the lost interests. On first day of eighth lunar month in 758, the court issued an imperial edict to suspend the Daisozu post of Jianzhen to let him specialize in expounding Buddhist texts. It seemed as though the court had let Jianzhen free from the busy official affairs, but in fact it was done under the influence of old guard. Emperor Junnin still carried on the tradition of respecting Master Jianzhen and conferred the title of "Daikasho-i (rank of Great Master)." The edict emphasized

对寺院也有规定，不供养外来僧侣，不供养不相识的僧侣；即使偶尔供养，也只限三天，三天之后，食宿自理。

757年十一月，朝廷下诏，以孝谦天皇的名义，将位于备前国（今冈山县）的水田100町（面积单位，1町＝9917平方米）赐给唐禅院，供养四方来学习戒律的僧侣，并且指定这100町的收入不受东大寺统管，由鉴真亲自处理。有了固定收入，唐禅院的宗教活动也就日渐活跃起来。但来唐禅院学律受戒者日渐增多，百町收入也只是杯水车薪，不敷应用。入夜，唐禅院的墙外总是有一些前来听法的可怜的僧人，因无处投宿，卧地而眠。另外，唐禅院寄人篱下，终非长久之计。因此鉴真决定设法建造一个规模比唐禅院大得多的中国式寺院，凡是来寺里学习修行的僧徒，一律免费提供食宿。他亲自进宫，请求朝廷的支持。圣武太上皇非常认可鉴真这一想法，遂将一处亲王的旧宅赐给鉴真新造寺院。鉴真将毕生致力于寺庙建筑的丰富经验和设计理念全部倾注于新寺院的建筑，集中了中国很多寺院建筑的精华。759年八月，新寺落成，淳仁天皇颁赐敕额"唐招提寺"，孝谦太上皇亲自为佛殿

唐招提寺建成后日本各地僧俗纷纷前来请益。《东征传》绘卷。
Monks and laymen in Japan seeking advice after the Tōshōdai-ji Temple was built. Panorama of *Voyage to East*.

that all circles of people should respect Jianzhen, and other temple monks and nuns should came to Jianzhen's Zen-in to study Buddhism.

Hearing this, the feudal officials and monks came to comfort Jianzhen, who was calm as usual. He thought he would introduce the Chinese culture to Japanese by focusing on promoting Buddhism irrespective of the post he took. In year 761, he presented his plan to construct an altar at both the Kannon-ji Temple and Yakushi-ji Temple, which constitute three altars together with the Todai-ji Temple. After this,

日本孝谦太上皇所题唐招提寺匾额。田建国
供图。
A horizontal board inscribed by the Japanese
Empress Koken. Photo credit: Tian Jianguo.

书写了匾额，同时宣旨：凡出家人必须先到唐招提寺研习律学，方可自选宗派。为了解决唐招提寺的经费，朝廷又颁赐田地75町作为寺产，供养僧侣。

唐招提寺成为日本第一个向外来僧侣提供食宿的寺院。一年四季，四方佛徒聚集于寺中。凡来唐招提寺学习的僧徒，除学律、受戒外，鉴真还向他们传授医药知识、建筑造像艺术，让他们抄写经书，学习汉语。唐招提寺成为一所传授中国多种文化知识的学校，学人之多盛极一时。弟子学成后，便成为一方讲授律学的名僧，可谓桃李满天下。唐招提寺也随之名声远扬，和奈良当时著名的官寺东大寺、兴福寺、大安寺并列，成为日本僧侣向往之地。唐招提寺的做法，是把封闭的、局限于上层统治阶级工具的佛教，逐渐改变为开放的、面向广大劳动人民的宗教。这在日本佛教的发展史上是一种重大改革。

only ordained monks became formal monks at the Todai-ji Temple, Kannon-ji Temple or Yakushi-ji Temple.

The Buddhist sutras brought in by Jianzhen enriched the collection of Japanese Buddhism sutras—specifically the newly-translated *Hua-yen Sutra* (80 volumes), which began the transmission of *Hua-yen Sutra* in Japan. Most of the sutras in Japan were from China or Corea by means of dictating versions. The dictated sutras had low reliability due to many errors. The court knew that Master Jianzhen was a well-read man of noble character and entrusted the task of correcting these sutras to him. Though blind, Master Jianzhen had corrected most of the errors on the Japanese sutra by his prodigious memory.

After the sea voyage eastwards, Jianzhen and his prentices including Situo expounded the Buddhist texts for the Japanese monks. Master Jianzhen explained the Buddhist sutras for Japanese monk Ninki and others, who were good at Chinese language, and trained a number of Buddhist lecturers. They later took part in the promotion of Buddhist sutra. A foundation of mitzvah study was set up and it changed the view of Japanese Buddhism. Master Jianzhen became the founder of Japanese Vinaya sect.

In the spring of year 763, monk Ninki, a prentice of Master Jianzhen, dreamt that the beam of lecture hall was broken off. Prentices believed this dream warned of the death of Master Jianzhen. They felt very sad and drew three por-

　　唐招提寺落成后的第二年，遣渤海使小野回国时，给普照带回来一个甍，上面写明是送给普照的。只知道是从唐土经渤海送到日本的，却不知道到底是谁送的。"甍"是安装在寺庙屋脊两端的鸱尾。这是一件古物，中间有很深一道裂缝。普照依稀记得这种形状，好像是在他居留唐土期间见过的东西。是在到大唐初期在洛阳居住修行的大福先寺，还是在长安期间居留的崇福寺，抑或是居留扬州期间的大明寺，都记不清了。这件东西引起了普照深深的感慨。他想起和荣睿一起度过的最艰难的岁月和最危险的途程，想起自己从一个20岁的年轻僧人到40岁的中年名僧难忘的日子，当然还想起在鉴真大师身边的幸福和快乐。他想，一定要把这件从唐土送来的珍贵鸱尾安装到一个恰当的地方。后来普照请人把它安装在唐招提寺金堂的屋脊上，每次来这里，总要感动地凝望许久。

　　日本佛教是官僚化的佛教，是天皇贵族的统治工具。鉴真初到日本时，他的授戒方法从根本上控制了私度为僧的混乱局面，缓和了僧侣人数的激增，因而与天皇的指导思想一拍即合，得到了天皇的全力支持。而鉴真想让佛教给受苦受难的百姓带来精神慰藉，把大多数

唐招提寺藏宝阁。田建国摄。
The Tōshōdai-ji Temple's Treasure House. Photograph by Tian Jianguo.

traits of Master Jianzhen in different angles to retain his image. Three portraits seemed not enough, and they molded a seated statue of Master Jianzhen with lacquer and hemp cloth interlayer technique by Situo.

On sixth day of fifth lunar month of year 763, Master Jianzhen passed away at the age of 76 in the posture of sitting cross-legged and facing the direction of his motherland. His face was calm and firm with a drop of tear trickling down the eyes…

The death of Master Jianzhen shook the court. Feudal officials, monks, nuns, and common people came to Tōshōdai-

民众作为传戒弘法的对象，这种想法与天皇朝廷以佛教控制百姓、巩固政权的指导思想却大相径庭了。于是，天皇朝廷中的保守派便对鉴真日渐冷淡。圣武太上皇去世后，孝谦天皇禅让皇位于淳仁天皇，鉴真也就失去了最有力的支持者，于是朝廷中少数保守势力和旧教团中的顽固派便乘机蛊惑淳仁天皇，妄图夺回已经失去的权益。758年八月初一，在孝谦天皇让位时，朝廷下诏，停止鉴真大僧都的职务，令其专事讲经传律。表面上看这是朝廷让他摆脱烦杂行政事务的羁绊，但其实质是旧教团势力的影响。淳仁天皇还是继承了尊崇鉴真大师的传统，尊其为"大和上"。诏书同强调指明，对鉴真要恭敬供养，让他专心致志讲经传戒，诸寺僧尼，欲学戒律，就要到鉴真大和尚的唐禅院去。

天皇诏书颁发后，日本官员和僧人纷纷到东大寺唐禅院安慰鉴真，鉴真却是心地坦然，谈笑如常。他认为，只要专心致志地讲律传道，无论是不是担任大僧都照样可以将中国文化介绍到日本民众之中。761年，鉴真又启奏朝廷，在西国观音寺（筑紫）及东国药师寺（下野），各设戒坛一座，与东大寺合称为天下三戒坛，举行传戒。此后，无论何人，若不受戒于东大寺和

唐招提寺御影堂外观。日本TBS供图。
Exterior view of the Miedo Portrait Hall, Tōshōdai-ji Temple. Photograph by TBS, Japan.

唐招提寺御影堂内日本画家东山魁夷手绘屏风。日本TBS供图。
Hand painted screen by Japanese painter Kaii Higashiyamain Miedo Portrait Hall, Tōshōdai-ji Temple. Photo credit: TBS, Japan.

下野药师寺、筑紫观音寺，便不得成为正式僧侣。

　　鉴真东渡日本带来了抄写的各种经疏，大大地丰富了日本佛教经藏的传播。特别是自鉴真带去新译的《华严经》80卷，日本才开始有《华严经》传入。另外，日本的大量经典都是从中国或高丽口授译文传抄过来的。口授译经本身质量就不高，传抄过程中又常常出现讹误。日本朝廷得知鉴真"博涉经论，尤精戒

《黄山晓云》
Seas of Clouds in Huangshan Mountain

《涛声》
Shiosai

唐招提寺戒坛。田建国供图。
Kaidan of the Tōshōdai-ji Temple. Photo credit: Tian Jianguo.

ji Temple to express condolence. Both Japanese and Chinese monks were deeply grieved. The Tōshōdai-ji Temple and Todai-ji Temple held all kinds of activities mourning for Master Jianzhen—the Chinese monk, who made great contribution to Japan. His tomb tower was built on an island dotted by pine and cypress trees and encircled by a river within the Tōshōdai-ji Temple. No precise record existed on the death of Fusho, who made great contribution to Jianzhen sea voyage eastwards.

After the death of Jianzhen, the Japanese officials, litterateurs, monks and nuns, wrote many poems in praise of him. In August (lunar calendar) the year after his death, the Japanese court sent people to temples in Yangzhou, hometown

律"，便将校正一切经典的重任委托给他。双目失明的鉴真凭他惊人的记忆，校正了大量当时日本佛经传写中所发生的讹误。

东渡日本之后，鉴真不但自己广泛讲授律学经疏，他的弟子思托等人也经常为日本僧人讲授戒律。鉴真还反复为通晓汉语的日僧忍基等人讲授律宗经典，培养了一批律学师资，后来他们都在各地寺院进行传律活动，大大树立了戒律的尊严，奠定了日本律宗的基础，改变了日本佛教的面貌。鉴真也成为日本佛教律宗的开山祖，被奉为"扶桑律宗太祖"。

763年春，鉴真的日本弟子忍基做了一个梦，梦见唐招提寺讲堂的栋梁折断。弟子们相信预兆，认为这预示着鉴真大师将不久于人世，便在悲伤中为师父准备后事。他们为将师父的形象留在世上，为他画了三幅不同角度的坐像；但又觉得不够，便由思托以干漆夹纻法塑造了一尊鉴真大师的坐像。

日本天平宝字七年（763年，唐广德元年）五月初六，鉴真结跏趺坐，面朝西边祖国的方向圆寂，终年76岁。弟子们看着鉴真安详、坚毅的面容，似乎有一滴清泪从师父的眼窝里渗出……

Lacquer and hemp cloth interlayer technique

The technique was used to produce Buddhist images by painting lacquer on hemp cloth brought from China in late 6th Century. The artwork is passed down to today by the Japanese handicraftsmen from generation to generation. A rough core was first modeled in clay and then layers of hemp cloth soaked in lacquer were applied over the surface with each layer left to dry before adding the next layer. Some required decades of layers. A wooden or bamboo framework was fitted inside the statue to prevent warping. When the lacquer layer was dry, the clay core and the framework were removed, forming a lightweight hollow statue. It was very popular during the times of Sui and Tang dynasties as it was easy to get materials and produce big Buddhist statue. The statue of Master Jianzhen in Tōshōdai-ji Temple in Nara was made using this technique.

of Jianzhen, to inform the bad news. Monks of temples in Hangzhou sunk in great sorrow and wore mourning dress to wail in mourning for three days facing the direction of Japan. The people held grand memorial for Jianzhen at the Longxin Temple where Jianzhen lived for a long time. Later, the Longxin Temple caught fire. Only the room Jianzhen lived was safe without any damage. What a miracle!

In year 799, 16 years after the death of Master Jianzhen,

干漆夹纻法

干漆夹纻技法是一种将漆涂于麻布表面使其干燥成型的制作技术，约于6世纪后期由中国传入日本，历代日本师匠精心钻研，流传至今。干漆夹纻佛像用泥巴塑成型，内用木或竹作支架，然后蒙上纻麻布，敷上一层漆，再蒙上一层纻麻布，有的要敷上十几层。待漆干透凝固后，再除去内中的泥巴和支架，它既坚固又轻巧。由于它取材容易，又能造出大的佛像，故而在隋唐时期十分流行。供奉在奈良唐招提寺中的日本国宝鉴真大师坐像就是运用此种技法的杰作。

日本朝野震动，官员纷纷前往吊唁，闻讯前往唐招提寺吊唁的僧众更是不计其数。奈良诸寺僧侣和随鉴真东渡的中国僧人都悲痛万分，在唐招提寺和东大寺分别举行了各种隆重的佛事悼念活动，超度这位功勋卓著、道俗归心的中国和尚。鉴真的墓塔建在唐招提寺内一个河水环绕、松柏长青的小岛上，让奔波操劳一生的大师安静地长眠。为鉴真东渡立下了汗马功劳、奉献了毕生精力的普照圆寂于哪一年，史料没有

Mahito Genkai, a popular Japanese writer, finished the *Eastward Expedition of a Great Monk in the Tang Dynasty* in accordance with the book on biography of Master Jianzhen written by Situo—a prentice of Master Jianzhen. It was very precious to the world as it retained the immortal achievements, his words, and moral character.

确切的记载。

鉴真圆寂后，日本人民用多种形式歌颂其光辉的一生。官员、文人、僧尼写下了大量诗文，歌颂鉴真的不朽业绩。鉴真死后的次年八月，日本朝廷特派遣使臣，专程到鉴真故乡扬州的各个寺院，告知大和尚圆寂的消息。扬州寺院僧众得到鉴真圆寂的噩耗，悲痛万分，全部穿戴丧服，脸朝东方，面对日本方向举哀三日。人们还在鉴真长期居住过的龙兴寺举行了盛大法会，表示对鉴真的深切怀念。后来龙兴寺毁于大火，只有鉴真住过的房子完好无损，令人称奇。

779年，即鉴真大师圆寂16年后，日本著名作家真人元开根据鉴真弟子思托撰述的《大唐传戒师僧名记大和尚鉴真传》，写成了《唐大和上东征传》一书，为后人保留了鉴真大师的不朽事迹和音容笑貌，弥足珍贵。

VI

Benefactor of Japanese Culture

A part from propagating Buddhism and imparting its commandments, Jianzhen brought the valuable Chinese culture to its neighboring country Japan. He made great contributions for the development of Japanese culture. For this reason, he was called with respect: "Benefactor of Japanese Culture," "Ancestor of Japanese Religious Circle," "Forefather of Japanese Medicine" and "the Holy Monk."

The Tang Dynasty during Jianzhen times was the Golden Age of temple architecture. Yangzhou, the hometown of Jianzhen, has over 40 huge temples. The architectural style of temples found something new in what is old, absorbed, and merged with the artistic style of Western countries, Persia, and even Byzantium. Digging into the Buddhist scriptures, Jianzhen attached great importance to the art of temple architecture. He involved in constructing over 80 temples in China before going to Japan. He also built countless statues of Buddha, designed and took charge of

6

文化恩人

　　鉴真在日本除了弘扬佛法、传律授戒，还将绚丽多彩的中国文化传播到一衣带水的邻邦，为日本文化的发展作出了杰出的贡献。他因此被日本人民尊为"盲圣"、"日本医学之祖"、"日本的文化恩人"。

　　鉴真所处的盛唐时代，寺院建筑艺术已发展到鼎盛时期，单是鉴真的故乡扬州就有较大的寺院40余所。寺院的建筑风格也在推陈出新，吸收和融合了西域、波斯乃至拜占庭的艺术风格。鉴真在钻研佛教经典的同时，也注意研究寺院建筑艺术，在东渡日本之前就参与建造寺院80余座，造佛像无数，或设计或主持施工，可谓建筑造像大师。他到日本不久，就奉天皇之命在东大寺建造了戒坛院和唐禅院。后来又建造唐招提寺，鉴真是建筑这座寺院的设计师和总指挥。

the temple constructions. Not long after he arrived in Japan, he constructed the Kaidan-in Hall and the Tang Buddhist Temple. He constructed the well-known Tōshōdai-ji Temple too.

Many rooms in the Tōshōdai-ji Temple were reconstructed based on the original old buildings, of which "Kondō" (Golden Hall) was the most exquisite building during the Japanese Tempyo era. It was a rare architectural treasure. Most of Kondō of Japanese temples were constructed with double decks, but the Kondō of Tōshōdai-ji Temple adapted a unique monolayer structure. Its design was based on the form of temples during the Tang Dynasty period, and absorbed the advantages of foreign architecture designs. The

唐招提寺千手观音立像。 田建国供图。
The standing statue of Thousand-hand Guanyin in Tōshōdai-ji Temple. Photo credit: Tian Jianguo.

唐招提寺金堂。田建国供图。
The Kondō in the Tōshōdai-ji Temple. Photo credit: Tian Jianguo.

　　唐招提寺的许多房舍都是利用原有的旧建筑改建的，其中的金堂被认为是日本天平时代最为精美的建筑，是不可多见的建筑艺术珍品。当时日本寺院的金堂多是双层构造形式，唯有唐招提寺的金堂采用了与众不同、突破传统的单层形式。它的设计既取范于唐朝寺院的造型，又吸取了外国建筑的长处，佛殿最前面的圆柱游离在外，别具一格，外观既华美又庄严，有一种和谐的美感。日本学者将其评价为"今日所存

column to the foremost of the hall has a distinctive style, with gorgeous and majestic appearance, reflecting an aesthetic feeling of harmony. The Japanese scholars appraised it as the "most complete hall of the temple in the Japanese Tempyo era. Its structure and ornamentation represent the most popular architectural style during those times."

The statuary art in the Tang Dynasty was flourishing, and it inspired many talented Buddha gravers. The Yangzhou statuary art had developed to a highest level during the Han Dynasty, and entered a period of maturity during the Tang Dynasty times. The artistic and aesthetic values of idols carved in wood, molded in clay, and exquisite jade carvings and dry lacquer statues are very high. Jianzhen

唐招提寺内日本俳圣松尾芭蕉名句碑。俳句内容为："嫩叶滴翠,摘来拂拭尊师泪。" 田建国摄。
Matsuo Basyo's famous Haiku stele in the Tōshōdai-ji Temple. It says, "Pick a green young leaf to wipe off Master's tears." Photo credit: Tian Jianguo.

天平时代佛殿之最完备者；其构造装饰，足以代表当时最兴盛之式样手法"。

唐招提寺金堂卢舍那佛坐像。田建国供图。
The seated statue of Vairocana in the Kondō, Tōshōdai-ji Temple.
Photo credit: Tian Jianguo.

唐代的雕塑艺术已相当发达，佛像塑造高手如云。鉴真的故乡扬州早在汉朝时雕塑艺术就已发展到较高水平，到唐代已经步入成熟阶段。扬州的佛像除了泥塑木雕外，还有雕工精美的玉雕和干漆夹纻造像，其艺术价值和美学价值极高。鉴真和他的弟子思托等人都是造像高手，在鉴真东渡的随行工匠中，又有雕塑师、玉作人、绣师、画师等。唐招提寺落成后，鉴真带领他们和参加唐招提寺建造的日本工匠一起，在寺中造了卢舍那大佛坐像、药师如来立像、千手观音像、梵天像、帝释天像和四天王像。其中金堂内的卢舍那佛坐像是日本现存干漆夹纻雕像中最大、

153

and follower Situo and others are all statue masters. The artisans accompanying Jianzhen included sculpturers, jade craftsmen, embroidery masters, and painters. After completing the Tōshōdai-ji Temple, Jianzhen and these craftsmen built the seated statue of great Lusena Buddha, standing statues of Yaskushi Nyoral, Thousand-hand Guanyin, Brahma, and Four Heavenly Kings in the temple. The seated statue of Great Vairocana Buddha in the Kondō is the biggest and the most majestic dry lacquer statue existing in the Japan. After the dry lacquer statue was used by Jianzhen, such statue became prevalent in Japan. These statues in the Tōshōdai-ji Temple have provided good artistic source for the spread and development of Japanese statue art thus becoming the gem of such arts in Japan.

Jianzhen was proficient in medicine. He cured Japanese monks coming to study Buddhism when propagating Buddhism in Japan, and taught them Chinese medical knowledge. Jianzhen had cured the Empress of Japan from chronic illness. He identified the medicines took by the Empress and found out a counterfeit drug. A lot of drug ingredients in Japan were imported products, and it was difficult to distinguish between the true and counterfeit drugs. The Japanese government invited Jianzhen to identify the medicines. Although Jianzhen lost his eyesight, he was able to identify drugs based on smell, taste, and hand touch. Since then, the Japanese government made

最宏伟的一尊坐像。自从鉴真采用干漆夹纻造像之后，这种造像艺术在日本盛行起来。唐招提寺的这些佛像为日本造像艺术的传播与发展提供了很好的艺术借鉴，后来都成为日本的传世艺术瑰宝。

鉴真本人精通医药，他在讲律传戒期间，曾亲自为前来学习的日本僧徒治病，并将中国的医学知识传给他们。鉴真曾为久病缠身的皇太后治病，效果极好。鉴真为她诊断之后，又将皇太后服用的药物一一鉴定，发现其中有一味假药。日本当时的许多药材都是舶来品，真伪难辨，于是日本朝廷委请鉴真对日本的药物一一加以鉴定。当时鉴真虽双目失明，但他靠嗅觉、味觉和手感能准确地辨别药物的真伪。此后日本就以药袋印有鉴真像的为真药。直到江户幕府时代（1603—1867），日本的药袋上还印有鉴真的肖像。鉴真亲自带到日本的"奇效丸"、"万病药"、"丰心丹"等几乎成为日本民间的常备药。日本直至14世纪以前，凡从事医、药两道者，都将鉴真奉为始祖。

鉴真对日本的绘画、书法等的发展也有杰出的贡献。唐代是中国绘画艺术突飞猛进的时代，寺院、崖窟、墓葬中壁画盛行。鉴真东渡时便带有画师、佛

medicine bags with the head portrait of Jianzhen printed to show real medicines. The medicine bags had the portrait of Jianzhen printed on it until the era of Tokugawa (1603–1867). The "miraculous pill," "medicine curing all diseases," and "Fengxindan" became the common medication in Japan. Jianzhen was regarded as the forefather of medicine before the 14th century.

Jianzhen made outstanding contributions towards the development of painting and calligraphy in Japan. The art of drawing made astounding advances during the Tang Dynasty period, and the wall painting was prevalent in

temples and for graves. The Tōshōdai-ji Temple has three rooms with wall paintings. Patterns of grass and dragons with flames were put on the back of statues. These paintings become a model for Japanese painters contributing significantly towards the development of Japanese art of painting.

Chinese calligraphy was introduced to Japan in earlier times, but it became prevalent in Japan only after Jianzhen went there. Many Buddhist scriptures brought to Japan by Jianzhen were hand-written copies of the Chinese

赵朴初 (1907 – 2000) 题签鉴真纪念碑。乐敏供图。
The Jianzhen Monument inscribed by Zhao Puchu. Photo credit: Le Min.

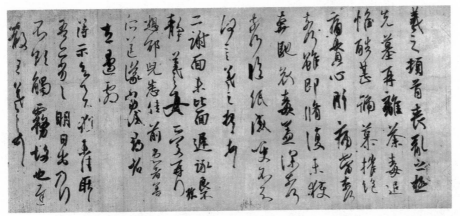

传鉴真带到日本的东晋书法家王羲之行草杰作《丧乱贴》、《二谢帖》、《得示贴》，唐朝摹本，三帖厚于一纸。张恕供图。
Wang Xizhi's *xing* (walking)-style calligraphic works probably brought to Japan by Jianzhen. Photo credit: Zhang Shu.

画，唐招提寺内也有三间壁画，一些塑像的背后有唐绘中常见的唐草与火焰抢珠图案。这些绘画艺术成为日本画家学习的范例，对日本绘画艺术的发展影响很大。

中国书法传入日本较早，但盛行中国书风还是在鉴真东渡之后。鉴真带入日本的大量佛经都是手抄的，本身就是中国书法作品。经过日本僧侣的传抄，书法唐风也便随之盛行起来。鉴真东渡时还带去了中国书圣王羲之（303—361）、王献之（344—386）父子等人的书法真迹 50 多帖，成为日本书家的楷模。

另外，鉴真和他的弟子在日本都是用汉语讲学，

calligraphy works. After the Japanese monks copied them, the Tang-style calligraphy was in fashion. Jianzhen brought over 50 pieces of calligraphic works created by Wang Xizhi (303–361), and Wang Xianzhi (344–386, seventh son of Xizhi), who were called Chinese "Saints of Calligraphy." Their works became a role model for Japanese calligraphers.

Jianzhen and followers gave lectures in Chinese, making the Japanese learn Chinese language extensively. They popularized the Chinese knowledge, and made the Japanese people absorb Chinese culture easily. Jianzhen brought Chinese printing and colourful cooking culture into Japan.

Today, both the Chinese and Japanese remember Jianzhen's role and great efforts in facilitating the culture exchange between them. In the Tōshōdai-ji Temple, the seated statue of Jianzhen sculptured by Ninki and Situo still exists. In Yangzhou, the homeland of Jianzhen, and in the Daming Temple where he lived and delivered lectures, the Jianzhen Memorial Hall stands tall. The famous Chinese architect Liang Sicheng (1901–1972) designed the hall based on the design of the Kondō in the Tōshōdai-ji Temple in 1973. Artists of Yangzhou sculptured the statue of Jianzhen (based on the statue of Jianzhen of the Tōshōdai-ji Temple) using nanmu preserved in the Forbidden City. Guo Moruo (1892–1978) inscribed "Monument of Jianzhen Monk of Tang Dynasty" on a huge marble plaque. The Monk Jianzhen's Sails Eastward Monument stands on the Baota Bay, southern

鉴真坐像、弟子思托塑。唐招提寺御影堂藏。田建国供图。
The seated statue of Jianzhen, carved by his disciple Situo, housed in Miedo Portrait Hall. Photo credit: Tian Jianguo.

使日本僧侣广泛学习汉语，大大普及了汉语知识，为古代的日本人民吸收中国文化提供了很大方便，对日本汉文字的发展也是一个推动。还有人认为，鉴真亦将中国的印刷术和丰富多彩的饮食文化传往日本。

今天，中日两国人民都没有忘记鉴真在中日文

suburb of Yangzhou. Langshan of Nantong City set up a monument to commemorate Jianzhen's journey eastwards. Sanya City of Hainan Province—Zhenzhou—from where Jianzhen failed to set out on his fifth journey, has a monument for Jianzhen's landing. The cliff has a group of statues of Jianzhen and his followers.

Jianzhen lived in Japan for 10 years. The Saga Prefecture is the place where Jianzhen landed. It has a monument depicting Jianzhen's landing. The Todai-ji Temple of Nara City has a Jianzhen statue. The Tōshōdai-ji Temple and the Kondō, precious deposits, collection of sutras, figure of Buddha and Jianzhen statue are on the list of Japanese treasures under special protection. Some temples with deep relationship with Jianzhen are preserved and kept under special protection, i.e. Todai-ji Temple, where Jianzhen had lived; Sennyu-ji Temple, where Jianzhen was given Dharmagupta-vinaya by his follower Komatsu; Kofuku-ji Temple, where the Japanese monk Yoei had lived; Daian-ji Temple, where Fusho had lived; the octagonal nine-storey pagoda in the Saidai-ji Temple constructed by Jianzhen's disciple Situo. The historical novel, *The Roof Tile of Tempyo*, written by Japanese writer Yasushi Inoue in 1957, represents the great accomplishment of Jianzhen's journey eastwards. "The roof tile of Tempyo" refers to Jianzhen, who just like the Shachi-hoko on the roof tile, represents the top of Japanese culture during the Tempyo period.

化交流史上的伟大功绩。在鉴真主持修建的唐招提寺里，至今还供奉着鉴真弟子忍基和思托塑造的干漆夹纻的坐像。在鉴真的故乡扬州，他曾生活和讲学的大明寺建有鉴真纪念堂，是由中国著名古建筑学家梁思成依照日本唐招提寺金堂设计建造的。纪念堂内的鉴真雕像，系依照唐招提寺供奉的鉴真塑像，采用北京故宫珍藏的楠木雕制而成，后来又依照唐招提寺的鉴真像重塑了一座干漆夹纻塑像。堂前的巨型大理石碑雕刻着郭沫若亲笔手书的"唐鉴真大和尚纪念碑"。在扬州南郊宝塔湾鉴真东渡造船登舟的地方，立有鉴真东渡纪念碑。南通市狼山也立了鉴真东渡纪念碑。海南省的三亚市，即鉴真第五次东渡失败登陆的振州，建有鉴真登陆纪念碑，山崖上还有鉴真东渡一行的群雕像。

鉴真在日本生活了十年。日本佐贺县是鉴真东渡登陆的地方，立有鉴真大和尚登陆纪念碑。鉴真到达日本后，住过的奈良东大寺内供奉着鉴真塑像。鉴真主持建造的唐招提寺以及寺内的金堂、宝藏、经藏、佛像、鉴真和尚像都被列为日本国宝，受到特别保护。一些与鉴真大师因缘很深的寺庙，如鉴真最早居

Mediated and promoted by Deng Xiaoping (1904–1997) in 1980, Morimoto—abbot of Tōshōdai-ji Temple—visited China carrying the paint dry seated folder of Jianzhen. The Daming Temple in Yangzhou was reconstructed and a grant memorial ceremony was held to carry forward Jianzhen's greatness for his journey eastwards. In honor of Jianzhen, a luxurious cruise named "New Jianzhen Ship" shuttles between Shanghai, China, and Osaka and Kobe, Japan.

住的东大寺，他的日本弟子小松道传授鉴真大师《四分律》的泉涌寺，邀请鉴真东渡的日本留学僧荣睿居住过的兴福寺，普照居住过的大安寺，鉴真弟子思托所建的西大寺八角九重塔，以及药师寺等，都完好地保存下来，今天仍受到政府的重点保护。日本现代作家井上靖于1957年写成历史小说《天平之甍》，再现鉴真大师的东渡伟业。"天平之甍"指的就是鉴真大师，意思是，他就像屋顶上的那块鸱尾（甍）一样，代表了天平时代日本文化的最高峰。

1980年，在中国领导人邓小平斡旋推动之下，唐招提寺住持森木孝顺奉鉴真干漆夹纻坐像回国"探亲"，扬州大明寺得以重修，举行了盛大的纪念仪式，使鉴真东渡的伟大功业得以弘扬。为纪念鉴真大师，现在往返于中国上海和日本大阪、神户间的豪华游轮，就命名为"新鉴真轮"。